DREAM KEYS
FOR LOVE

**Unlocking
the Secrets
of Your
Own Heart**

LAUREN LAWRENCE

A Dell Book

Published by
Dell Publishing
a division of
Random House, Inc.
1540 Broadway
New York, New York 10036

Dell books may be purchased for business or promotional use or for special sales. For information please write to: Special Markets Department, Random House, Inc., 1540 Broadway, New York, NY 10036.

Dell® is a registered trademark of Random House, Inc., and the colophon is a trademark of Random House, Inc.

ISBN: 0-440-23478-6

Printed in the United States of America

Published simultaneously in Canada

December 1999

10 9 8 7 6 5 4 3 2 1

OPM

To my parents, Jack and Elaine,
and to my son Graham

ACKNOWLEDGMENTS

I am immensely grateful to Raoul Felder for debriefing a number of his divorcing clients of their dreams. Profuse thanks to those others who generously and openly shared via their dreams whatever their hearts and minds were feeling during or after their divorce or severing relationship, especially to Liba Icahn, Ivana Trump, Jennifer Grant, former Secretary of Commerce Robert Mosbacher, Anthony Quinn, Chris Royer, Janice Dickinson, Cameron, Laura Hunt, Carolyne Roehm, and Mai Hallingby. A note of thanks to my prolific dreamer and dressmaker Katie Stephanatos.

Special thanks to Brooke Astor for revealing a most poetically poignant and self-critical visitation dream wherein she is reprimanded by her deceased grandmother, to my friend Geoffrey Bloomingdale for sharing a visitation dream of his father, and to my beautiful friend Carmen Dell'Orefice. Heartfelt appreciation to Soheir Khashoggi, Dewi Sukarno, and Ghislaine Absy for sharing profound dream intimacies.

A debt of gratitude to my agent, Liz Berney, and my editor, Diane Bartoli.

Lauren Lawrence
New York, N.Y.
September 9, 1999

Gain New Understanding of Yourself and Your Relationships Through the Amazing and Revealing Nature of Dreams.

Discover:

* How divorce or breakup dreams of men and women differ: Men dream of buying things, women dream of re-decorating the home.

* Ways in which self-affirmation dreams provide the strength to carry us through tough times. Share super-model Janice Dickinson's empowering dream during her custody battle.

* How understanding anxiety dreams of abandonment and rejection can help you raise your self-esteem.

* How relationship dreams reveal what went wrong in a relationship.

* How dreams of children of divorcing parents can be used to help them express their fears and feel more secure.

* How when you dream of emerging from water, it's a symbol of rebirth and your own ability to survive. Check out supermodel Beverly Johnson's inspiring dream.

* How a visitation dream of a loved one can bring peace. Read the wonderful words spoken by Dodi Fayed to his aunt in a dream she had after his tragic death.

* PLUS—Classic dream symbols including: climbing stairs (sex), falling (surrender to erotic temptation), losing a tooth (castration in men, pregnancy wishes in women), mist (blurred reality or missed longing for what is gone in the phonetic sense), music (passions), naked-ness (truth), party (celebration of life), spiderwebs (entrapment), storm (stressful time), train station (departure) . . . and much more

DELL BOOKS BY LAUREN LAWRENCE

Dream Keys

Dream Keys for Love

CONTENTS

FOREWORD

))

According to scientists, everybody (even animals) dreams, or at least all mammals do. In the seventeenth century, the Spanish dramatist and former priest Pedro Calderon de la Barca declared, "All life is a dream," which may explain why he was a *former* priest. These two thoughts, taken together, suggest that our nights are composed of dreams within dreams. If the riddle of life remains unsolvable or, perhaps more correctly, so incapable of any approach toward comprehension that the magic solution of religion is leaped upon as a life raft in a stormy sea, at least our nightly excursions into a dreamworld are an attainable choice for exploration.

An ancient Hebrew proverb says, "A dream that has not been interpreted is like a letter unread." And speaking of ancient Hebrews, the Bible, of course, was very big on the interpretation of dreams, beginning in Genesis, "And we told him, and he [Joseph] interpreted to us our dreams; to each man according to his dream he did interpret," on to the New Testament, which speaks of "false dreams," and "old men [who] shall dream dreams." Given the fact that dreams have been the stuff of human preoccupation since ancient times, and in light of today's stresses, it is entirely fitting and proper that dream exploration continues. And, unfortunately, it is all too often the demons that pay us nightly visits—visits that reflect the problems of our awake lives.

The navy developed a "stress table" in which, by some process, a Richter scale of the stresses one meets in life was formulated. The list includes everything imaginable from receiving a traffic ticket, to having a fight with your boss, to the serious traumas of life. At the top of the list is death of a loved one. The next most stressful event is divorce. And there are those who argue that death should have been number two and divorce number one since the former is an event one cannot control and the latter one that is beset with "should haves" and "would haves."

In answer to Detective Polhaus's question, Sam Spade pointed to the Maltese falcon and explained, "This is the stuff of dreams." Dr. Freud was more on target when, in *The Interpretation of Dreams*, he quoted Lucretius, "And whatever be the pursuit to which one clings with devotion, whatever the things on which we have been occupied much in the past, the mind being thus more intent upon that pursuit, it is generally the same things that we seem to encounter in dreams, pleaders to plead their cause and collate laws, generals to contend and engage in battle." In short, and with less eloquence, people who are in the throes of a failing marriage have their dream life occupied with this unhappy circumstance.

Lauren Lawrence has collected and interpreted the dreams of the divorcing. In a population whose marriage *failure* rate hovers around 50 percent, and whose actual *divorce* rate is about 30 percent, it is remarkable that no one has ever before done this. In Ms. Lawrence's pages I see specific clients and adversaries I have met throughout the years. The consistency of universal themes is striking and the interpretations reveal much about the people themselves.

Whether the interpretation of the dreams will reveal "the

small hidden door in the most intimate sanctum of the soul," as Jung suggests, or merely let one know what he or she is in for, this book is a "must-read" for the divorcing or unhappily married.

Raoul Lionel Felder

PREFACE

For the most part, love relationships break down because of inappropriate behavior patterns that go unrecognized in our daily lives. Because we simply lack the time, objectivity, and distance required to deconstruct and analyze a situation when we are in the thick of an interpersonal altercation, our lives are often saturated with misapprehensions of events. Unfortunately, it is far easier to pass blame and draw false conclusions than to penetrate beneath our defenses—our personal propaganda—which is why every intentionally biased view has its emotional appeal.

But personal recognition has its own attraction . . . in that if we learn what we have done wrong (or what was done wrong to us) in a love relationship we will neither be condemned to suffer the dismal consequences of repeating our past mistakes nor any longer permit the indignities of subservience and abuse. We will not have to assume the roll of either victim or victimizer. This desperately needed nonpartisan personal recognition may be gained through dream interpretation in that the best way to examine our troubled selves is by analyzing our objective unconscious dream. Thus, it may be said that dream analysis sprays a unique brand of Windex on the blurred mirror of denial as it clarifies our rearview mirror of the past . . . sometimes disclosing a past we never dared imagine to be true.

There are many types of dreams that convey the emotional devastation brought about by severed relationships whether through divorce, relationship breakups, or death. Each of these categories of separation or dissociation cause dreams that specifically relate to the circumstances of the terminated relationships. *Dream Keys for Love* Parts I and II examine and record the numerous and varied dream motifs pertaining to love gone wrong in order to clarify the prevailing range of maladaptive feelings that often necessitate protective or remedial action on the part of the divorcing or divorced individual. In other words, I have tried to show through dreams the characteristic and sometimes gender-based responses of a divorce upon the psyche, as these dream motifs reveal to the dreamer the different attitudes and unconscious reactions to the trauma of the divorce event; other dream motifs such as burying the head dreams, dreams of being lost or abandoned, or dreams of being killed off/identification with parent's pain examine how divorce impacts on children. A new concept of actualized dreams demonstrates how depressed or divorced spouses often act out their fantasies in *conscious* but unrecognized dream states that negatively manifest themselves through physical action and behavior presentation.

Part III exemplifies from a psychological framework the meaning of five typical love visitation dreams of the deceased, wherein dreamers incorporate the deceased into their lives so as to reestablish or breathe life back into the former relationship as a means of consolation, warning, instruction, inspiration, or prophesying (intuiting) the future. A paranormal perspective examines the possibility that the unconscious mind is a conduit to the world of spirits wherein love visitations *are* real.

The interpretations of the dream narratives within the text indicate the vast knowledge of the unconscious mind and verify the dream process as a hermeneutic tool for reconstructing a higher quality of life. Hopefully, *Dream Keys for Love*, through its fifteen typical divorce dream motifs, will define and demystify the nature and gender differences of divorce responses and the ill effects divorce has on the self in a way that will enable the reader to understand the aftermath of divorce—its accompanying pain, anxiety, and sense of failure—and get beyond it.

Part IV dedicates itself to breakup dreams and examines the five major reasons a love relationship fails. It ponders (through dream interpretation) what went wrong within a partnership that started out so right. In that breakup dreams are impartial, they cannot be overvalued, as they often reveal who did what to whom with the intention that the information gained be used as a measure of what not to do again so as not to repeat former mistakes.

On a personal note, throughout the book I have presented and analyzed numerous breakup dreams that map out the landscape of error in failing or failed relationships with the hope that these dreams will allow readers a shared intimacy with their contemporaries who have gone through the splitting experience of love gone wrong.

Most important, it is my intention that inferences will be drawn as to the reliability of dream analyses for forecasting a relationship breakup before it occurs and that these inferences will provoke inward examinations of readers' own dreams with the goal of salvaging their relationships.

PART I

**Troubled
Love
Dreams**

1

The Traumatized Psyche

To understand the traumatic effect divorce has on our psyche and more specifically how the divorce process impacts differently on the male and female dreamworld of the unconscious, it is necessary for us to examine how divorce was historically viewed and received throughout the centuries.

Ingrained somewhere within our vast collective social consciousness, we can still hear the trenchant resonating voice of the Catholic Church campaigning throughout Western society . . . the chorus of condemning bishops . . . the denouncing sermons of fist-pounding priests vilifying divorce. So frightening was divorce that a mere mention of the word shivered the secular spine of humanity from the dismantling vision it evoked: The earth would shake from *a parting of the ways* and bring the steam-powered wheels of the family system to a halt. Let's face it, if divorce was an ugly word, untying the knot was a Herculean feat certain to leave rope-burn.

The Church presupposed but nevertheless believed that the social harmony gained through marriage set the cornerstone of a social hierarchy delineated by the purest form of community known to man—the family. It was thought that the lack of this family system—a structure based on female spousal obedience and marital indissolubility—as caused by divorce would bring about the destructive effects of social turmoil and pave the way for a conflict-ridden class society. Even as late as in the nineteenth century, progressives and conservatives alike recognized that marriage and the family were fundamental social institutions and that social change or the maintenance of the prevailing social order could not be achieved without preserving the family.

Interestingly, the first written divorce regulations that many early societies followed were found in the ancient Babylonian Code of Hammurabi, which permitted *only* husbands to get a divorce. Such was the extent of male superiority that Jewish weddings incorporated into their ceremonies the veiled threat of divorce via male spousal dissatisfaction: The glass that is broken by the groom (although primarily a symbolic reference to a destroyed temple) is meant to remind the conjugal "couple" that marriages can also break if not protected. Poignantly, it is the groom that stomps and breaks the glass with his foot . . . never the bride . . . as though the glass (an obvious feminine symbol) is an obstruction underfoot! It is precisely this recurrent male/female polarization that manifests and insinuates itself into the psyche in the form of dream motifs.

In the Middle Ages after Charlemagne's spirit rode off into the dust of his own history, married women were regarded as useful pieces of property, although of frail constitution. The husband being granted full authority over the property his wife owned at the time of the marriage may explain why many men think and dream of divorce in terms of ownership—of buying and selling. In what I call the *pasha mentality,* divorce was granted if a husband was discontented with his wife's dowry, personality, or with the yield (not just agricultural) of her land—euphemistically tilled to propagate!

One can only imagine the blight, not to mention the stain on the apron of the emotionally guilt-ridden female psyche which as we shall see distinguishes itself in the dreamworld by presenting symbolizations of socially enforced female inferiority—the home, as a representation of the female persona, is often dreamt of as being in a state of disrepair.

In these bleak ages of gender inequality, where domesticity was almost always tied to femininity, it seems that years of being excluded from areas of social and personal achievement (except in the role of wife) have taken their toll on the collective, subjugated, male-dependent, housewife-mother female psyche. Of recent years, analytic sessions are still filled with the disenfranchised sounds of divorcées who have lost their sense of individual importance—a significance gained through spousal identity—pondering their sense of isolation, anonymity, respectability or the lack thereof, trying to discover their sense of purpose and self-worth. Such is the unconscious shame—the dreams of responsibility!

It is easy to comprehend that breaking a marriage vow traumatizes the system, and that a historically male-biased society impacts differently on female and male consciousness. But the answer is yet to be given to the question that must be raised: Does untying the knot produce heartache (and all manner of unsettling dreams) because society frowns on divorce or because the love one feels for a spouse is no longer returned or even received? Perhaps the heartache stems from what is psychologically known as infantile primary narcissism, which cannot abide *separation anxiety* . . . anxiety over the loss of the caregiver, the primary love object? Whatever the answer, the heartache and trauma of divorce—in the legal sense or otherwise—continues to effectively trouble the world of our dreams.

2

Heartburn or
Separation Anxiety

The actual meaning of divorce can be visualized in the psychologically significant scene near the end of Woody Allen's *Annie Hall,* the unbearable moment when Alvy realizes that his relationship with Annie is over. Putting his car in gear Alvy inadvertently moves forward, hitting trash cans with a loud crash, then while backing up his convertible he purposefully smashes into the side of a car that has just turned into the parking lot. He then drives his car full force into another parked car and, in reverse, rams his convertible into the front end of yet another car. Sirens blast and drivers rush out from various cars yet Alvy stays seated, firmly entrenched behind his wheel . . . waiting for the motorcycle cop's approach.

Whereas marriage is being parked in the parking lot in the space reserved for you, divorce is having to leave that space, and after banging all the other cars on your way out, realizing that there is no space quite right for you any longer. The anger at having to leave the sanctity and security of the parking lot is not as troubling as the fact that at the moment you have nowhere else to go. *There is no space reserved for you!*

We know that sooner or later inadvertently going forward in a bad relationship will almost certainly set you up for a crash. Banging into any oncoming obstacles in your path signifies both your anger—certainly your lack of vision—and lack of power and mastery over the environment or situation. You feel great vulnerability to harm in a world now conceived as being dangerous and hostile. So why stay firmly entrenched behind your wheel, flirting with disaster? Because you are territorial? Because you want what you can no longer have? Possible answers both, but more than likely you are having a flashback of *separation anxiety*.

In contemplating divorcing or breaking up, we may recognize the same situation as that which underlies our first great state of anxiety at birth—separation anxiety. The infantile anxiety of longing, not to mention the accompanying indignant cry of horror, that results from a separation from the omniscient mother—the primary caretaker who selflessly nurtures and protects—is surely enough to make one belly-crawl straight back to the womb for some high time intrauterine experience. As our fragile egos interpret living as meaning the same as being loved and protected, divorce is a process of separation somewhat akin to dying in that it is bound to stimulate in the unconscious the sense of abandonment by all protecting forces—the sense of being unloved.

This form of anxiety is commonly found in divorce dreams of loss and/or dislocation because the divorce process is a process of becoming detached and separated from another entity. This process cannot help but recall our backward glances on the first day at nursery school, lunchbox tightly in hand, our trepidation engendered by the fear of separating from our loving mother. To some extent, going through a divorce is like letting go of the *motherhand* as it allows the self to feel deserted by all protecting forces (present lawyer excluded) and allows the self to temporarily flounder like a fish out of water because it believes itself incapable of succeeding by its own strength. This is a fear about letting go, opening up, and trusting oneself not to fall apart like a house of cards in the wind.

But separation anxiety does not necessarily imply that any great love has been lost in the divorce transaction, in the splitting from the significant other. Separation anxiety is what a cat feels when it has no itching post—or when it lacks warmth from the absence of a hot-blooded human to rub up against! To a certain extent the umbilicus has been cut and requires that major adjustments be made as to how, when, and where the next meal will be arriving.

As the divorce process is a trauma to the system, a turn of events that reintegrates within our lives that primal fear of abandonment, it produces longing accompanied by despair. Given these circumstances, mature adults often become anaclitic infants overnight and often rapidly turn dreams into nightmares. Emotional independence is no longer believed in or accepted and is temporarily replaced with cherished remembered thoughts of sublime dependency.

Separation anxiety acknowledges that external help is needed to survive and produces the same traumatic situation of helplessness in the divorcing adult as in the child who longs for and is distressed by the absence of the maternal presence. Herein, the missing primary love object or caretaker (reintegrated into the psyche as the spouse) is interpreted as a loss of the object's love. This loss of love translates into a sense of abandonment brought about by feelings of personal worthlessness and undesirability. The ego of the noninitiating divorcing spouse, particularly when another lover is involved, shrinks to little less than a quark.

A GENDER'S VIEW OF SEPARATION ANXIETY

Whereas the male child has feared the danger of castration and thus in later life is interested in supplementing and buttressing his fortress and property (a positive goal, I might add), the female child has feared the danger of abandonment (or some sort of mental castration). In her later life the stress once laid on the danger of losing the love of the loved object (now perceived as the spouse) becomes explicitly related to female sexuality and is perceived as an ego threat (desirability and self-worth crumble in the process). The absence of the mate makes self-preservation a feminine issue, and in most cases an economic upheaval follows an emotional one. To be sure, this gender difference manifests itself in the midnight reveries of our psyches in that divorce dreams seem to be formed on the basis of socio-emotional prototypes. Whereas women dream of internal physical dissolution, men dream of external acquisition (see Anthony Quinn) and moving on (see Robert Mosbacher). Whereas women find fault within themselves via personal attribution (see Mai Hallingby), men exteriorize the divorce as situationally derived and apart from themselves. Women collapse whereas men run off to encounter new adventures.

Society places certain expectations on its members through the roles they are required to play in regard to commitment. Marriage places demands on the wedded or socially accepted couple—demands that a divorce dissociates them from. But when the sense of identification or commitment is lost through the self-protective process of withdrawal (distancing oneself) or intellectualization (denial of responsibility) the person must pay a price in low morale, impaired social functioning, and even damage to health due to stress.

Divorce violates a social expectation as it creates role ambiguity, and without role clarity one is unable to plan effectively or to behave in a directed, purposeful, goal-oriented manner. In that divorce temporarily eliminates the chance for our emotional demands to be met, we often revile ourselves with disapproval and self-loathing, which threatens our ability to belong and therefore endangers our prospects of gaining the social advantages we require to lift our sagging spirits.

POSTPARTUM DEPRESSION

A prominent factor in female depression that is caused by divorce is the void the spouse leaves. This spousal void may be likened to postpartum depression but whereas postpregnancy blues are quick to dissipate because of the mother's proximity to and association with birth, new life, living, becoming, purpose, and growth, the divorcée senses an absence similar to death, for in a sense an individual identity has been destroyed, dismantled, or deconstructed. Divorcées that have internalized their spouses will suffer from a loss of identity and self-worth—one might say a deficiency of their maleness, their ego strength.

Separating from the spousal object forces the divorcée to become individuated. Many female divorce dreams deal with identity motifs. Figuratively, the *he* has been removed from the *she,* leaving the lonely sibilant *s,* which when pronounced on its own makes an audible sound of disgust coupled with disbelief.

HEARTBURN

Whereas heartburn develops in divorcées who still feel altruistic, selfless, romantic love for their no longer visible spouses (wherein the act of loving is more important than being loved in return), separation anxiety develops from selfish dependency—the continuation of early narcissistic patterns of gaining gratification from the tender ministrations of the primary love object. Many divorcing couples experience a mixture of both heartache and recidivistic need. But wherever the emotional angst is derived from, one thing is certain—divorcing couples badly need Alka Seltzer!

The unconscious medicates with its uplifting bubbles of alkaline dreams that rise into consciousness and emulsify the emotional acidity. Releasing our divorce dreams into consciousness brings us one giant step closer to understanding our innermost feelings—our traumas, our disillusionment, our nagging guilt or sense of dissolution and futility, which we have oftentimes assiduously and defensively repressed even from ourselves. It is time to let the fizzing begin.

The very process of divorce makes one look at life through a diffraction glass that dismantles, shatters, and splits every remembered image into fragmented representations. Divorce is the time to bring on the bulldozers—there is deconstruction to be done before we can rebuild. Just remember that men wear different hats and deconstruct differently than women.

3

Women Nest and Men Hunt: Separate but Not Equal

J erry Seinfeld once noted a profound behavioral sex difference between men and women in regard to their usage of the remote control for the television set—whereas women are content to stay tuned to what they are watching, men vigorously shift from channel to channel. Seinfeld ended his comedic monologue with the words "women nest and men hunt." No truer words were said particularly in regard to the psychological effects on the psyche of the divorcing couple as manifested in the unconscious world of dreams.

Upon reexamining the ending of *Annie Hall* wherein Woody Allen's character, the emotionally distressed Alvy, sits firmly entrenched in his car in the face of great odds, reaffirming the symptom of separation anxiety by seemingly not wanting to leave the security of the parking lot. It is time to focus on Alvy's strangely neurotic behavior. Importantly, it should be noted that Alvy's reluctance to leave his convertible should not in any way be confused with nesting. In that the car is a symbol of power and freedom, Alvy is simply recharging his male ego batteries. His sense of male desirability and dominance has just received the equivalent of getting an atomic wedgie, yet with his underwear and pride literally over the top his "boys" are out there, baby, and part of him is loving it.

A car, as an engine that heats up, is a symbolic representation of the male genitalia; in a symbiotic way the car inflates his momentarily deflated body part. Soon, we know that Alvy will be able to play the field again (even this cliché is male biased, for how many women do we know who play baseball?). The pain Alvy feels from being rejected by the woman he loves will be supplanted by his new freedom and the joy of purchasing powerful male toys that feed the ego—toys purchased with male money. The more money, the faster the car and the faster the weakened male imago revs up. The focus is on expensive cars, cigars, speedboats, the purchasing of large homes, stocks, and so forth—on investments in things external to the physical body. For buying is linked with ownership, and for the most part men view divorce as a loss of ownership rather than a destructive interactional situation that will disrupt their nonsubordinate role in society or minimalize their degree of self-worth and aggressive goal-oriented nature.

So, when men dream they dream big. They dream that they are buying when they are ready to sell! They chalk up their loss as one among many gains that will predictably occur during their lifetime—while all the while anticipating and believing in their future gain. Their physical persona is not minimalized or degraded for long.

Remote control in hand, they are on to a new channel. They set their sights to score anew—for men are hunters at heart. The male heart is a hunter with its finger on the trigger and the female is the target that keeps getting bigger.

While going through his divorce, Anthony Quinn dreamt of buying the right house (see Buying and Selling / Property Loss and Gain / The Male Imago). He had to choose between the one and the other, for by gaining one he would lose the other. Anthony's ownership dream will be analyzed farther along in the text.

Women on the other hand, nest—their house is who they

are. In that women often feel synonymous with the home and hearth, the divorced female spouse frequently experiences environmental upheaval, particularly when the husband is perceived as being the source of all nurturing and protective ministrations. But whereas this environmental junta of sorts should be situationally attributed, women tend to internalize the situation and make personal attribution. In other words, they own it. It is their fault.

Because women are physically symbolized by the home (after centuries of being regarded as nothing more than the homemaker) and as the divorce represents the breakup or destruction of that home which the women have internalized, dreams of falling apart follow closely upon the retreating heels of divorce.

In this transitional period in their lives, it is quite common for divorced or divorcing women to dream of their homes in disrepair, falling apart. Unconsciously the woman and not the home is falling apart. There is the need to redecorate, which symbolically refers to changes and alterations in physical appearance and reinforces a women's sense of undesirability. A new physical presence is sought.

Going through a nasty divorce the socialite Mai Hallingby (see dreams of Redecorating and Refurbishing the Home: The Female Imago) has had many recurrent dreams of homes that need significant work, dreams that reinforce how the sense of physical decline is intrinsically related to the emotional upheaval caused by the divorce. Windows are either broken or needed to take a long look out from. Radiators are poignantly missing as they symbolize the lack of emotional coziness, and dearth of human warmth from the loss of spousal love. The house needs repainting, a thicker skin is needed, and there is much to be covered over or whitewashed. The roof is falling in. There is no protection from the elements. Dissolution is everywhere with chaos the new tenant instead of order. Furniture needs to be purchased (dreaming of buying new chairs is the wish for stability and structure) as there is much empty space from the spousal void that needs to be filled.

On a more constructive note, dreaming of needing more space may also suggest that freedom and a newfound sense of being and identity are sought after—style is no longer cramped. The dream may fill the home with a party atmosphere wherein strange new men may appear wandering through the house, for a substitute partner must be found. The house needs maintenance of the spousal socioeconomic protective kind. The nest must be filled!

SEPARATE BUT NOT EQUAL

In conclusion, as we have seen, a parting of the ways separates the conjugal couple from shared ground but does not leave them on equal ground emotionally. Similarly, we have noted that the historical (one is tempted to use the word *hysterical* in its psychological usage) view of divorce is more than ample reason to ripple shock waves on the Richter scale of the unconscious. Whereas there is trauma for both sexes, the male gender-biased society has ensured that women, due to their historically subservient position, suffer more emotional upheaval during and after divorce, which results in dreams of a heartier, more energized form of anxiety.

PART II

**Defining
Your Dream:
The Three
Main Types
of Divorce
Dreams**

4

The Anxiety Dream

The anxiety dream may be viewed as a product of our having to live in what social scientists have previously termed the age of anxiety, presently thought of as the age of stress. These dreams are a shaky lot in that they anticipate the daily problematic annoyances of waking life and magnify all the dangers our tender flesh is heir to. They thrive on our fears, frustrations, worries, and conflicts—on our imagined inability to cope. Anxiety dreams occur whenever we feel overwhelmed or at a loss (particularly during divorce proceedings) because they focus on our insecurities rather than our strengths while holding us in the grips of the most dreadful situation or feeling. Yet, as opposed to being reflective, these dreams dwell on the future, on the what-ifs. As anxiety dreams tend to nail down the stressful realization that we are not in control of our lives they elicit subject matter of chaotic and even nightmarish proportions. Our unconscious is doing battle with something clearly unpleasant, disagreeable, and even unthinkable. With our intentions either frustrated, thwarted, or misunderstood, the editing of these anxiety dreams is usually haphazard and frenzied—the cinematic mood is one of hopelessness and dread.

The most significant feature of an anxiety dream is that the anxiety never ceases or is resolved during the course of the dream such that the dreamer often awakens in a sweat, feeling unnerved and on edge. Particularly angst-ridden dreams are those wherein spousal hate is directed toward the dreamer and wherein the spouse is viewed as a stranger and thus enemy (see Paranoia Dreams). There are certain anxiety dreams, however, that include falling, forgetting, losing, or disorienting motifs wherein the anxiety present often manages to resolve itself before the end of the dream. This has the effect of turning this type dream into one of wish-fulfillment or self-affirmation.

As mentioned earlier, a salient feature of anxiety dreams is that they focus on our insecurities, which explains why divorce dreams are always brimming with nail-biting anxiety— because the ego has never felt less secure. To the extent that any anxiety that occurs during the daily ministrations of life, no matter how seemingly insignificant, is received by our system—the filtering system of the unconscious—one can well imagine the anxiety produced by a socially negative life event that hammers in its own marker and flags the rupturing experience of divorce. The filtering system of the unconscious is similar to that of a coffee brewing machine. The superficial muck—the remains of the grounds—stays outside, while the undiluted liquid filters through to the realm of the unconscious, where it stays repressed.

Divorce taps into one of the most prevalent anxiety dreams—performance anxiety—because, in effect, divorce says, "I did not perform my conjugal duties correctly and was unable to make this relationship/situation work." When coupled with the harsh historical view of divorce, this is a heady brew of anxiety to leave percolating in the unconscious.

To the extent that the physical dynamics of splitting an object in two symbolically evokes wreckage, the emotional mind remembers separating or being pulled apart from something as being a painful and difficult process. Whereas a peaceful mind aligns itself with harmony and wholeness, it shrinks from the cacophony of schism, leaving that which is broken perceived as damaged goods. As damaged goods are viewed as worthless, severing emotional ties produces a lack of self-worth that often translates into feeling physically broke, or penniless. This is why anxiety over finances is particularly common in dreams of divorcing women.

After generously querying numerous clients for me in regard to this book, Raoul Felder, one of the most notable and articulate divorce lawyers in the country, has been able to substantiate that divorce dreams are always unpleasant, anxiety-provoking nightmares. The various dreams of Mr. Felder's clients seem to gravitate around the following themes: the fear of being impoverished (fearing an inability to maintain an accustomed lifestyle), the worry over an ex-spouse being paired with either a gorgeous woman or handsome man (someone perceived as being better than oneself), and the fear of losing children through custody battles (talk about *relative deprivation*!).

Thematically, it should be noted that all fears contained in the above-mentioned divorce dreams are concerned with the future as opposed to focusing on the here and now, which has the effect of nullifying the sense of presence of mind. One woman client who was living on Park Avenue repeatedly dreamt of being penniless. In her recurring dream she was no longer living at her present residence. (As a house in dreams symbolizes the self, the self in this dream has in some way vacated or been nullified, it is no longer living.) She had moved to York Avenue and was eating spaghetti, probably without sauce! (She eats to nourish her impoverished self, which has relocated and is thus modified.) As York Avenue is the last strip of land before the river, she is one symbolic step away from being in the river, floating downstream the way of the jilted Ophelia.

Another female client of Mr. Felder's dreamt that she was at a B'nai B'rith meeting when her ex-husband walked in with a beautiful young model at his side. Oh, the agonizing anxiety of it all! The dream revels in feelings of jealousy and betrayal but more important reveals undeniable feelings of divorce-triggered insecurity and undesirability. The dream is morbidly echoic of how women have been historically objectified as possessions that could be replaced (or worse, beheaded, as was the manner of choice of Henry VIII) when and if they were deemed fallen in value. The beautiful model promises great mileage like the new model car that the husband shows up with after having gotten rid of the old model. The dream imagery of the B'nai B'rith meeting symbolizes the divorcing spouse's loss of trust, in that B'nai B'rith is a Jewish organization that is associated with faith. The divorcée is betrayed at her place of faith. She can no longer go there for solace.

Another woman client dreamt that she had visited her children's school, only to find that her children no longer knew who she was. Whereas divorce irons new creases into the worrisome face of anxiety, it steamrolls over our selfhood, flattening our now featureless egos until we are unrecognizable even unto ourselves. By losing one's identity or place in the world the dream has turned the woman into a faceless nonentity. The divorced wife/mother, no longer independent within the confines of her marital relationship, has become dependent upon others. She has become needy (separation anxiety), and her neediness has produced within her the anaclitic child in want of the primary love object (her own mother) whereas her children (who are supported by the father/husband) are perceived as having moved on with no recognizable need to be double parented.

With the sense of family collapsing brick by brick the divorced wife has no definite role in society. Necessarily, the anxiety divorce dream is all about survival of the self and its departure from partnership in society at a time when the social self is feeling half of what it once thought it was.

AN INTUITIVE OR PROPHETIC ANXIETY DREAM

The following dream preceded the breakup of a Manhattan designer's marital relationship. **Katy**'s dream thematically reveals jealousy and anguish over her spouse's possible infidelity and amazingly intuits her husband's romantic involvement with another woman. The dream is as follows:

Looking into the room of my bedroom I suddenly saw my husband. I saw a big white mink coat sprawled across the bed. I saw another woman prepared to go someplace with my husband. I heard her say, "We have to leave." I could not hear where they were going. (Then I was awakened from sleep by the sound of the front door slamming closed. I walked around the apartment and realized that my husband had just left. I rushed to the window and saw my husband with a big suitcase, going into a white limousine waiting on the street. He had left for Las Vegas with a strange woman without telling me.)

What is fascinating about this dream is its intuitive nature. The dreamer has somehow sensed the departure of her husband simultaneous with his actual leaving, for he leaves both in the dream and in reality. It could be argued, however, that the sound of the door slamming is what causes the dreamer to rapidly link the sound of departure with her unfaithful husband, who had already metaphorically exited from the conjugal "bedroom" of trust and fidelity.

In that a room in a house symbolizes the person, the idea of another woman must have previously entered Katy's conscious mind as surely as another woman has entered her bedroom within the visualization of the dream. More specifically, the bedroom represents the marital union. Being outside the bedroom suggests that the dreamer is beyond the conjugal realm, on the outside looking in. Seeing and overhearing an event in which things are happening without her consent reveals that Katy feels she is in a powerless position. Outside of the marital loop Katy is at best a bystander to conjugal perquisites.

The big white mink coat is symbolically perceived as a luxury item that appears in actuality sprawled on the street transfigured into a waiting white limousine. Clearly, the fear of spousal departure from the home was already in Katy's unconscious, but it took a dream to allow Katy to suddenly see her husband and prepare her for what is to follow. As the dream states, the other woman *is* prepared whereas Katy is somehow at a loss. The many signals of marital dissolution and spousal unfaithfulness that may have been repressed during the dreamer's wakefulness have found their avid audience in the dreamworld.

5

The Self-Affirmation or Self-Empowerment Dream

The self-affirmation (or self-empowerment) dream starts out with problematic or distressing content, as in a typical anxiety dream, with the difference being that the dream takes a turn for the better. Miraculously, we are allowed to surmount whatever difficulty we are floundering in, to reestablish a faith in ourselves, in our sense of self. These dreams espouse women's gymnastic coach, Bela Karolyi's motivational approach—his "you can do it" jargon. Like those little plastic dolls in the backseat windows of cars, these dreams are the nodders, the insouciant yes-men. Inspirational and uplifting, they allow us to regain the illusion that we are in consummate control of our lives—that we can do the impossible.

These dreams are the thunderous hand-clappers that never cease to applaud our seemingly effortless feats. They accentuate the positive and squelch the negative. Affirmation dreams of this sort frequently include flying motifs, as they often endow us with Superman skills (cape and tights excluded), supernatural powers, and great strengths: we can leap buildings in a single bound, carry huge weights, move boulders, exist beyond time and space. Dreams with survival motifs are protective in nature (see Robert Mosbacher), as they manage to empower the impoverished spirit.

During and after divorce proceedings we need all the affirming we can muster because we have had our somewhat delicate sense of selves dragged around the blistery terrain of the courts by a lawyer's long leash. In that we have had to listen to impassive third parties deciding the domiciles of our future, it is wonderful when we are able to dream of darkened, cramped homes changing for the better—becoming more spacious and well lit (see Jennifer Grant)—in an attempt to affirm our self-worth and desirability.

The following self-affirmation or self-empowerment dream was dreamt by supermodel **Janice Dickinson** during court battles regarding her first marriage custody suit:

> *This guy I know turned into a Cherokee Indian with a beautiful, glowing Cherokee Indian face. (In real life he is a druggie.) He turned into an attorney. He told me nonchalantly, "I only make four million a day." He laid down on the floor to listen to the earth. He had long hair. I wanted him sexually and I wanted him to defend me.*

The guy that Janice knows who turns into a Cherokee Indian is none other than herself dreaming of becoming powerful (in reality, the beautiful, dark-eyed, raven-haired Janice resembles an Indian). Like Lady Macbeth fearing her feminine nature, Janice wants to be rid of the milk of human kindness. It is as though the dream states in Shakespearean manner, "Unsex me here." The Indian represents the warrior, his long hair a Samsonian power that Janice needs to connect with in her difficult present life situation of ongoing court battles. As Janice wants him sexually, she wants his sex (in that she wants his gender, wants to be empowered with his masculine Indian strength and fortitude).

More than anything else Janice's dream reveals her strong

need to be defended. And who better to defend Janice than an Indian who is also a successful attorney who makes four million a day, no doubt on the warpath in the divorce courts. The Indian is the empowerment of Janice. Janice's greatest strength is her belief in herself!

The Indian lying down on the floor to listen to the earth symbolizes Janice's wish to become grounded. Listening to the earth is listening to one's inner voice—what is beneath the surface—for spiritual nourishment. The guy described as being a druggie changes from druggie to successful lawyer in a form of transformation that Janice would like to master. Post-divorce, Janice is feeling weakened, dazed, and confused—under the influence—as she is most likely feeling manipulated or easily influenced by others.

In the middle of a custody suit, where a child may have to be forfeited, Janice is identifying with Native Americans who have had their land and property taken away from them. Janice is the Cherokee Indian on a warpath trying hard not to lose her child. The affirmative dream symbolism allows Janice to attain a measure of self-empowerment that will enable her to persevere during this difficult period in her life.

Importantly, Janice understood that she was the Indian and that the message of the dream was to convince her of her strength.

6

The Wish-Fulfillment Dream

Wish-fulfillment dreams come packaged with magic wands and should be stamped *satisfaction guaranteed* for they are the genie of dreams. They perform functions and are considered dreams of convenience. They fulfill desires, gratify, pacify, mend, placate, or exonerate. These dreams allow dreamers to do what they cannot do in wakefulness: the actor, Christopher Reeve, who is paralyzed from the neck down, has told Joan Jedell, publisher and editor of the *Hampton Sheet,* "In my dreams I go everywhere, I go on wonderful trips with my wife and children." Wish-fulfillment dreams may also include consolation dream motifs of visitations of deceased loved ones (see dream of Victoria Principal). Freud, however, makes the claim that most anxiety dreams are really wish-fulfillments that have been disguised and repressed. What is certain is that wish-fulfillment dreams make things happen. Above all else, the wish-fulfillment dream seeks to rid the dreamer of anxiety.

During a divorce many dissatisfactions need to be gratified. As a divorce weakens the bond—the sense of couple—there is often the wish for strength and power, the wish to regain what is perceived as missing (see Dreams of Longing). There is also the desire to control the situation or outcome (see Rescue Fantasy Dreams). In that a divorce often produces feelings of guilt over cause, there is often the wish to transfer the guilt elsewhere onto someone or something external from the divorcing spouse—the wish to make a situational as opposed to a personal attribution.

The following wish-fulfillment dream is interesting not only because it contains classic divorce imagery but in that it prefigured a divorce. It was dreamt by Edith Rockefeller, a daughter of John D. Rockefeller Sr., while she was separated, geographically rather than legally, from her husband and the tensions of her marriage during her two-year self-imposed exile in Switzerland. She had mentioned the dream to Carl Jung before embarking on a long analysis with the noted psychoanalyst. During the time of her analysis, Edith was once again separated from her husband and the numerous problems in her marital relationship. This time the separation would widen into an unbridgeable gulf between them that would result in a swift divorce.

Edith had told Jung she dreamt of a tree that had been struck by lightning and split in two. Whereas Jung had thought her dream a symptom of latent schizophrenia the dream was actually revealing in no uncertain terms her desire to split—to sever ties—with her husband, which is verifiable by her eventual divorce several years later. The lightning either symbolizes an electrifying idea—a powerful bolt from the blue (the unconscious)—or the wish for divine intervention. The bohemian Edith was figuratively struck by lightning at the force and ferocity of her unrepressed wish to divorce, to split something traditionally solid and rooted. The tree as both a representation of the male phallus (the trunk) and the female genitalia (the leafy area) is a symbol of the marital union that must be rendered asunder, to separate the male from the female, the husband from wife.

Dreaming of the split tree is a way of making divorce possible. The task is so frightening a prospect and one so difficult to achieve that divine intervention is needed. The wish of the dream is that the marital union be severed no matter what the ramifications. And what better external attribution is there? The fulfilled wish is that the split occurs as a result of nature's tempestuous whim and not Edith's emotional inability to cope with the tedious responsibilities and fidelities of the marriage bond.

PART III

**Fifteen
Typical
Divorce
Dream
Motifs**

7

Redecorating and Refurbishing the Home: The Female Imago

What is the home if not a representation of the person who lives in it? The home is the being wherein the inner self resides—the various rooms, the walled-in, private spaces of the psyche. For the home is both the starting point and end point of all our entrances and exits, the place where we store our possessions, our worldly goods. With a roof over our heads the home represents sanctity as it protects us from harsh environmental conditions, shielding us from the cold, indifferent, or even dangerous external world of strangers.

As homes are considered reflections of the personality, the more palatial the home, the grander the sense of self. Inextricably related to matters of family and hearth, the home symbolizes a sense of permanence, harmony, and security. The home is our nest and thus a feminine image in that it is associated with nurturing and mothering. Because it is connected in this way to the female imago, decorating one's home (feathering one's nest) is somewhat akin to beautifying one's physical attributes. This is why we find that the dreamworld often symbolizes the first signs of emotional disharmony by depicting a house in disrepair.

Most divorce dreams depict the house in shambles, with much work to be done, wherein the female dreamer is running around making alterations and repairs, and redecorating. As mentioned throughout this text, the house represents the being or sense of self of the dreamer, and a divorce symbolizes a divided house or a house in upheaval.

Divorces usually leave the dreamer feeling emotionally drained or detached, with feelings of remorse, guilt, failure, and lack of stability. The self-image, usually fragmented and in need of repair, often manifests itself in a badly run-down house, or a house that needs reconstruction or redecoration.

At the first sign of marital trouble, it is quite common for many females to dream about building new homes, or about redoing or fixing up their existing ones. The following (redecorating and refurbishing) home dreams were dreamt by the socialite **Mai Hallingby** during her divorce proceedings:

> *I'm in a house with people in New York. At a party, I don't know whether people are coming or going. But outside there was another house being built that was incomplete. A house I was trying to finish. There was fog outside—mist, so I didn't quite see who was out there.*

As a house symbolizes who we are and the lifestyle we lead, being at a party where people are coming and going represents Mai caught up in the frenetic social whirl of society. The first house is the social posturing of the external persona. The other house being built outside is the dream's disguise—for this is the internal, private realm where outside indicates separate. This is the preparatory part of Mai that needs more space. It suggests that something is under construction, in the works; this is a period of personal growth fostered by the divorce process.

The house is incomplete, as it is an ongoing creation. (It is currently without a husband.) There is underlying structure but it must be built upon, dealt with. Because things are a bit foggy, Mai doesn't have all the answers. The fog softens things and blurs the sharp-edged harsh realities of existence that snag us every now and then. But trying to finish the house shows determination and is self-affirming. The dream imagery shows, however, that Mai is on the verge of self-discovery and a self-acceptance of her new autonomy, visualizing what it is like to be free and living on her own. Not seeing the whole picture, she cannot quite see who is out there.

The dream asks the question: Is there a new relationship on the horizon? Thus, the dream is an attempt to view the outcome—because the fog lifts! (Perhaps Mr. Right is just around the corner.) Mai's second dream continues along the lines of major life reconstruction and is as follows:

I am in my home and I notice that the radiator needs fixing, and that the paint is coming off the walls. There was a steam leak or something. Then I start thinking of how I can spruce things up. I go to the window and I notice that someone has built a large house on my grounds which is blocking my view; and worse, they are extending a long awning in my direction. I see there is a woman standing by the window. She is staring at me. I am extremely annoyed that she has built her house on my property. Then someone comes in and brings me two dresses for a ball I am going to. Someone says that Kevin Costner will be there.

Once again, the home figures prominently in the dream, as it symbolizes the dreamer. The radiator needing repair refers to the absence of warmth in the home. The paint coming off the walls is a subtle reference to Mai being thin-skinned. She feels things deeply, which is why she has dreamt such a revealing dream. The steam leak is Mai letting out her anger, blowing off steam, which is an honest release and why she is now able to attempt to spruce things up.

The large house that has encroached on Mai's property is the other woman who has temporarily blocked Mai's view to the future. This woman has invaded the sacrosanct territory of the marital home. But not to worry, Kevin Costner (representing Mai's one-upmanship on her offending ex-spouse, and the wish to meet an incredibly handsome and exciting someone new) is reason enough to want to go dancing at a ball.

Sometime after her divorce, **Jennifer Grant,** daughter of Cary Grant and Dyan Cannon, had the following self-affirming home dream which being reparative, heightens the sense of self:

Talking with friends . . . I realize I've a date I'm supposed to make dinner for. I hurriedly go to this tiny and dark apartment. . . . I'm looking for candles to light up the place, but can't find any. My date arrives looking sad. I say, "Come in. I'll make you dinner." He says, "I'm not hungry." Can't figure out what to do for him. We hug. He leaves. I leave this little apartment and walk into this huge home realizing this is mine. The bedroom is done. I walk past this gorgeous living room, figuring what am I going to do with this space? Down the hall is a beautiful sushi bar and a glass hall with nature all around, trees and water. I leave the house through a nature trail. I arrive at a theater across from my house. A friend says, "Isn't it great they're still lining up for this film." I know I've seen it, and think I'm in it.

In that house and room symbolism usually represent the being, one's view of one's own life, dreaming of a tiny and dark apartment signifies a bleak period in Jennifer's past (most likely during the collapse of her marital relationship) that had her looking for candles to light up the place. This action indicates Jennifer's optimistic spirit as she tries to alter a negative situation that at the time could not be altered—candles are not found. The date symbolizes a commitment and thus probably refers to Jennifer's ex, who is offered dinner, perhaps the only nourishment that can be given him at this time. But as the spouse is not hungry he will not be sated. This points to some failure in mutual satisfaction (the sad realization that the marriage is not working) wherein the dreamer has conscientiously tried but cannot figure out what to do for him or the situation.

Hugging symbolizes a nonsexual, platonic relationship and suggests that Jennifer (in revisiting her divorce in her dream) is trying to make amends, thinking of her spouse's well-being and even seeking his forgiveness. Once the date leaves (the divorce is finalized), Jennifer exits the little apartment misperceived as her own (her sense of self), and revelation follows—her horizon is expanded.

The dreamer enters a huge home and realizes, *this* is hers, which indicates that a brighter view of life is not only hoped for but expected. Whereas the first home was tiny and dark, the new home is huge/gorgeous. As the home is symbolic of the personality, this is a self-affirmative assessment. Jennifer is overhauling and upgrading her self-image by creatively contemplating what she will do with the space, the void in her life.

Whereas the bedroom that is already done signifies that the dreamer is emotionally ready to be romantically settled in a new relationship, the sushi bar in the home symbolizes that the dreamer is self-sustaining. The glass hall, although figuratively reflecting the dreamer's openness to the world and to new experiences, also reveals the wish to be watched over or publicly viewed. The nature trail, the road of self-discovery that the dreamer is free to follow, inevitably leads to a theater showing a film she has already seen and is in, which suggests that the dreamer has pictured what she wants in life.

What better self-affirmation is there than having everyone still line up to see you. This is the kind of personal acclaim that not only affirms to the dreamer that she has made a correct career choice but also a correct life choice—her divorce was approved by all.

8

Buying and Selling / Property Loss and Gain / The Male Imago

There are many gender-based nonverbal sex differences. Females in our society seem to be historically viewed as the oppressed sex—women tend to be oriented toward others in an accommodating manner that includes sensitivity to feelings, nurturing, and expressiveness. Masculine traits, on the other hand, involve personal efficacy, self-assertiveness, and task accomplishment, as this is the male imago. Whereas men are considered the helpful sex, women are considered recipients of help. In that women take up as little physical space as possible (sitting with legs crossed), men are more expansive, usually sitting with both legs wide apart. Avoiding small movements, men exist in a world of space and freedom, unlike women, who must be demure and physically unimposing.

Women are more attuned than men to other people and to the immediate situation, which is why divorcing women feel like they are coming undone and men feel like they have made a bad business transaction. Due to a lifetime of subtle pressure to internalize cultural expectations, women identify themselves with the home, and to the extent that women tend to interiorize they dream of their home (as themselves) falling apart. In that men tend to exteriorize, they dream of buying a new home (as their new spouse).

The following buying and selling dream was dreamt by

Anthony Quinn while he was in the midst of his divorce proceedings. As we will see, although the dream reveals that Anthony had mixed feelings and some regrets about his divorce action, he is very much a scrutinizing buyer sizing up the situation with a choice of two homes. His dream is as follows:

I live on the edge of a placid lake. The house is not big enough. Behind me is a big stone ruined castle. I am trying to buy it. But as I walk through it I realize it is not practical for modern living as all rooms are off a long, long passage. But I am not happy living in the house while the ruined castle is behind me. I love the view from that castle. I walk through both houses, never at rest.

As legends often occur in medieval settings, the legendary Anthony Quinn has interestingly dreamt of himself in a castle. And there is drama, too. Whereas a placid lake symbolizes reflection and gives him a surface view of himself, being on the edge of this lake suggests that the dreamer is on the outside looking in. He is ready to take the plunge to find what lies concealed beneath the depths of consciousness: this indicates that Mr. Quinn is on the verge of self-discovery. The edginess, however, that precludes the peace and serenity that could be attained by the dreamer is externally caused—for there is neither one perfect house nor one perfect spouse.

As the dreamer's state of mind is usually represented by the home allotted to the dreamer, the home that is not big enough suggests a stifled, restrictive, or claustrophobic sense of being (Anthony needs room to roam). However, as women are regarded as the accommodating sex and Anthony's dream is all about accommodations, it is safe to surmise that the two houses may also symbolize the two significant women in Anthony's life: his divorcing spouse, and his wife-to-be. In as much as spatial relations also refer to time, the big stone castle affords the immortal and unalterable sense of permanence, stability, and eternal existence—Anthony's sentimental ties to his estranged wife. The stone ruined castle (ex-wife) is a fortification that has withstood the wrath of time but nevertheless is the worse for the wear.

In that the castle is placed behind the dreamer, it suggests the unseen landscape of the past (Anthony's estranged wife); the castle beckons with its memories and the dreamer loves the view. But recapturing the past is neither feasible, nor accessible, as all rooms are off a long, long passage of time that can no longer be accessed. Although the dreamer desires the cool remoteness and introspection of the castle, he cannot deny his ornamental ties to the practicalities of modern living (the benefits of youth).

Walking through two houses, the dreamer perceives two worlds: the world of the conscious and of the unconscious, and the different relationships of past and present. On another more poignant level, the two houses symbolize the divorce event, which has caused a division external to the dreamer— the ruination of his former home is behind him. Even though the two separate houses (female personas) would be better as one, they must stand apart, indicating female loss. Yet clearly where there is male loss, there is also male gain, for a man's home *is* his castle.

Seeking emotional resolution or self-justification, Quinn walks through the world of the dead (the past) and of the living (the present), never at rest, like the ghost in *Hamlet*—a kingly spirit come round to rectify a life situation.

The following buying and selling dream was dreamt by a middle-aged mogul named **Paul** who was contemplating divorcing his wife for a much younger woman:

I was at the auto show looking at all the new models. I was trying to get close to this red Porsche but there were many spectators. Finally I was able to see over the shoulders of this woman. The car was shining in the light. I moved closer to get a better look at the paint job. I was admiring the red leather seating when I saw a huge price tag on the front seat and was worrying that I could not afford it. But then I noticed, much to my surprise, that my pockets were bulging, stuffed with money.

Whereas female contemplation of divorce (a house divided cannot stand) causes socio-emotional havoc in the dreamworld, the male imago asserts itself by exteriorizing the situation and by dreaming up pleasant analogies that will aid in the decision-making. As the word *auto* also means self, the auto show is really about glorifying one's self-presentation. The new-model cars are women substitutes in that they objectify women as something that is showcased or displayed— passing fancies whose value decreases in time. (To the extent that a man drives a car he directs and manipulates the action.)

The cars are sexualized, as they can be entered. Yet, getting close to a new red Porsche (a gorgeous young woman and/or model) is difficult because of the perpetual competition from other spectators or interested males on the prowl. This troubling idea necessitates ego boosting, which the dream is only to happy to supply in full measure.

There is the unmistakable feeling of dominance as Paul looks over the shoulder of a woman who is symbolic of his spouse, as she serves as a minor obstruction, albeit not an insurmountable one. There is no sense of marital fidelity as the woman proves unable to block his view. The only drawback to purchasing the new model appears to be the affordability. The paint job is scrutinized (given a closer look) in a manner that belies the dreamer's perception—the Porsche (woman) requires high maintenance!

Paul's pockets are bulging because he is sexually aroused by thoughts of ownership of a flashy new car (new woman). In that the pocket (a heart symbol) is stuffed with money, the dreamer is ruled by things material (property/ownership) as opposed to things spiritual—the emotions. Most important, the act of contemplating divorce does not make Paul dream of falling apart at the emotional seams but rather reinforces his masculine desire for freedom and space, revs up the motors of his ego and boosts his sense of self-worth.

9

Paranoia
Dreams

Paranoia in its deepest sense is really about whether or not one's perception of reality is to be trusted. It is defined as a delusional state wherein one irrationally feels either persecuted or glorified. But one is only paranoid to the degree that one's claims of persecution and/or glorification are illogical and unreasonable.

Paranoia dreams exist to the degree that nonpathological errors of judgment figure prominently in divorcing individuals whose sense of conviction as to the suitability of their respective mates has been dashed. I only mean to suggest that the dream possesses a peculiar psychic disposition, in that the dreamer becomes paranoid over things that the individual cannot in reality put up with.

In paranoia dreams whatever unconscious hatred is present in the individual is projected or displaced outward onto the object of the hatred. In the case of divorce dreams, this object is the divorcing spouse. Similarly, these dreams are seen as a mode of defense in that thoughts of violence that would normally trigger self-reproach often turn to distrust. Frequently in dreams, ideas of violence (toward the divorcing spouse) are projected or referred outward onto the divorcing husband or wife wherein the dreamer is forced to take protective action. As we shall see, the following paranoia dream contains such protective action. The dream that occurred during the height of Manhattan attorney **Angela B.**'s court battles is as follows:

> *My soon-to-be ex and I were on this jagged rocky cliff high up where it was difficult to keep one's footing—to keep from falling off the cliff. He was stabbing at me with a knife, trying to kill me, and I was bleeding all over the place—and I was stabbing him back to protect myself. Somehow I managed to kill him. I thought he was dead but I wasn't quite sure though. . . . Then these people (these two guys in white coats) came with an ambulance to pick me up because I was bleeding. They put me in the back. I was lying down. They were going through traffic but something seemed wrong. I wasn't sure if they were ambulance drivers or not . . . it was creepy. Then someone let me know that they were really agents of my ex-husband. I was trying to get out of the ambulance. There was a policeman outside. I was starting to go to him for help but then I wasn't sure if he was real or not. I was pondering if he was really what he was supposed to be . . . if he would help me or not. Then I awoke.*

Within the dream it is difficult to keep one's footing, in that during a divorce it is hard to stand firm and maintain one's balance, or one's ground, as the first thing that usually dissipates is one's natural sense of equilibrium. The very setting of the dream depicts a morbid image of the precarious nature of divorce and the vulnerability invoked by nearing the edge of a precipice in one's life. Teetering on an emotional brink of disaster, this is a marriage on the rocks!

With the elements of trust and protection gone from the marital relationship female spouses often fall prey to irrational fears—a paranoia based on vulnerability. At first subservient, the dreamer is repeatedly stabbed, penetrated by a phallic substitute knife and most probably linguistic death blows, verbal attacks on one's personal integrity. There is a paranoia that the divorce process will take away or kill off one's identity. The bleeding symbolizes the therapeutic of the past, bloodletting, as there is much that needs to be healed. The blood is also the menses, whose vivid presence assures the dreamer that no new birth will come from this relationship.

To the degree that Angela mimics the stabbing action of her divorcing husband, she is like him in a way that is most unsettling, which is why she will have to kill him in order to break the link. In managing to kill her ex-spouse Angela rids herself of male domination, which is perceived as a threat to her survival and demonstrates an assertion of will. In fighting back, Angela is no longer the victim, as she has established control over the situation and thus over her life. But in that divorce demonstrates the transitive quality of the marital relationship, suspicions arise and what is purely visual cannot be trusted (Angela is not quite sure her husband is dead). Things are not as they are supposed to be, which is why the symbol of a gun-wielding policeman becomes linked to an aggressive, dominating male presence whose imago is perceived as threatening or bad.

In that the act of divorcing poses its unanswerable question "How could I have been so wrong about my ex-spouse?" the dreamer begins to doubt her powers of judgment and inference. Metaphorically, she is driven to paranoia and even craziness by the ambulance men who arrive wearing white coats. The guys who arrive are not necessarily doctors and not necessarily here to help her heal, but they are nonetheless men, eligible men, which is why Angela is wary and even paranoid that they are agents of her husband. The men are viewed as members of the same team—agents of the same biological gender and therefore not to be trusted.

Angela is not certain if the policeman is real, as she is questioning sincerity and motives. But in the end it is not so much a question about whether she will be helped or not but about whether or not she will accept the help. By accepting help from a man, Angela would be accepting her own helplessness and proving the maxim that women are the recipients of help, which is perceived as being dangerous. Therefore, she must set about diminishing the policeman's role and power by questioning the nature of his authority, for in so doing she is also questioning the authority of men in general.

Another paranoia dream was dreamt by **Liba Icahn** during her divorce proceedings and is as follows:

I dreamt of a pig that was in the middle of the room. The pig was being poked and prodded by all these men that were surrounding it. It seemed that they wanted to skin it alive.

At the time of this dream Liba Icahn, wife of the billionaire corporate raider Carl Icahn, was going through divorce proceedings. She had already been to several lawyers, answered numerous questions, and gone through innumerable pages of documentation.

While the pig represents the succulent animal that can be cut up and portioned out—Carl Icahn's wealth—it holds another meaning. The pig, as an animal that grovels, symbolizes the sensitive Liba's own unconscious view of herself, promulgated by her innate sense of the male power structure she is up against, and is a sad indication of the female guilt involved in the divorce process, particularly when there are huge sums of money involved and prenuptial agreements that bind a fair allocation of funds. All these men are the opposing lawyers who have been poking away at Liba's sense of self-worth, at her very existence, accusing her of greediness. Going through this depersonalization process involves some serious mudslinging, which is why Liba's unconscious has dehumanized her into a pig, soft, pink, and most probably squealing about the wrongs of society—that this is a man's world. The dream reflects a social consciousness of female inferiority.

The pig is also viewed as the divorce itself—succulent and juicy. With whetted appetites the lawyers are readying their knives and forks.

10

Identity and Rebirth Dreams

The self-image is a by-product of an infinite number of social interactions with others in which the individual sees similarities to or dissimilarities from itself. The resultant self-image represents one's status as a member of a social group in a social system, which is why identity dreams often occur before or after major life changes: marriages, divorces, deaths, new occupations, or geographical relocation, during a time when the dreamer is seeking deeper self-knowledge.

Whereas the concept of identity is based on association and connection to an experience, identity dreams refer to an identity crisis—a self-estrangement in which the individual's self-image changes or is altered. These dreams often reveal role confusion over a new role or lack thereof. In that a divorce takes away one's role as spouse the self becomes somewhat less than what it thought it was; its credibility and propriety are somehow weakened, the role is no longer distinct. With the spousal role no longer clear, visibility is poor and self-recognition dim. Lacking self-esteem and self-worth, the ego frequently turns introspective and self-critical.

As the divorced spouse confronts the dramatic changes taking place in his/her life wherein intimacy with a significant other is broken off, the spouse may suffer from a sense of isolation and aimlessness. As emotional stress can disrupt one's self-image, it is safe to say that divorce can cause spousal disorientation whereby answers are looked for in a socio-emotional world that is no longer fathomed. It is the sense of selfhood that gives our lives a continuity that divorce deconstructs.

Frequently divorced or divorcing individuals feel no longer attractive, desirable, or wanted, to the point where they are ready and willing to contemplate a change of appearance—often going through physical transformation via change of hair color, hairstyle, dress style, and even plastic surgery. The following identity dream was dreamt by **Liz Berney** during the hurtful and tedious process of her divorce:

> *I was looking for a business card, and going from place to place looking at the different types of cards, the different colors. At first I kept looking at the traditional color ecru background with lots of small black lettering. The card would appear to me in my mind with lots of information on the card. Then I saw this card and I just started smiling. This was my card! It was my favorite color blue, a blue sky with white clouds and my name in the middle in white.*

Looking for a specific business card that expresses the integrity of the personality behind the card is symbolic in that cards are paper thin and pressed flat—the emotions of one going through the process of a divorce. The card as carrier of information symbolizes the need for self-recognition, identity, and self-worth—senses of self-image that dog-ear at the edges during stressful periods in one's life.

Looking for the right card is crucial for one's game plan, as the card represents a personal statement about strength (using your trump card), honesty (having your cards on the table), hidden agenda (having an ace up your sleeve), savvy (playing your cards right), and sanity (as in not playing with a full deck).

Looking at the cards with the small black lettering is a direct reference to the divorce proceedings—the dreamer must remain aware of the fine print. Not choosing a traditional card means the dreamer is permitting herself greater freedom of expression and creativity. When the dreamer finally finds her card she is overjoyed; it is sky blue with white clouds and her name is in the middle in white. Thus, she deifies herself by putting her name up in the sky. With her identity crisis over, the dreamer is able to spread her wings and rise in a flight of self-affirmation. The color white symbolizes purity of intention and enlightenment—starting anew with a clean slate—a paper version of a tabula rasa.

In that the divorce event represents the death of a relationship—the dissolution of a union, the end of a couple—it precedes a bleak period of mourning in isolation, wherein the divorced self withdraws within its own containment in a defensive effort to become whole again in order to attain self-completion.

Once again, in that identity is associative in nature and connected to an experience or role that brings about self-recognition, becoming alienated from the primary spousal relationship deprives the I of being unified through its behavioral and attitudinal physio-emotional dialectic of identification with the other. In other words, with the married I (eye) metaphorically closed, the single I (eye) must relearn how to see—how to revision itself.

Dreams with rebirth motifs are wish-fulfillments in that they represent the wish for a new life, a new beginning. The following rebirth dream was dreamt by the supermodel **Beverly Johnson,** just after her divorce:

This little baby had fallen in the water, in really dark water. I was afraid I wouldn't be able to hold my breath to get it. I dove in and brought the baby up, and the baby was not breathing. I gave the baby mouth-to-mouth and the baby started breathing again.

This wish-fulfillment rebirth dream works hard at summoning up the courage to bring something back from the depths. The baby is the reconstruction of the self after the divorce. The baby getting lost in the really dark unreflective water reveals the dreamer's sense of isolation. Being submerged in dark or deep water represents trouble brewing. The self-image is floundering on its own—perhaps drowning in a bout of self-pity. But something is salvaged, brought to the surface, and made accountable, as holding back breath underwater essentially means not swallowing or accepting a situation. (This situation is the death of identity—the death of the marital persona.)

The rescue of the baby succeeds because Beverly dives in head over heels in a spontaneity beyond emotion or reason and in a true creative spirit that places a value on creation and birth. Symbolically phrased, *I brought the baby up* means "I raised myself"; this is Beverly's way of reminding herself that she can make it through any difficult time and be self-sustaining.

The baby does not breathe at first which means that the baby is not taking anything into itself—is not incorporating any exterior experience. But there is the wish to resuscitate as the baby is affectionately given mouth-to-mouth in a courageous and loving confrontation and there is rebonding with the self wherein Beverly revitalizes her life and jump-starts the heart into pumping again. (There is life beyond divorce!)

The motifs of falling, becoming lost or displaced, and be-

coming small, helpless, and defenseless are found in dreams
in which the dreamer is recovering from some emotional upheaval (divorce is a deconstruction that requires reconstruction, for one must start from scratch to build anew), by
reclaiming, refinding, rebirthing, and reenergizing—all of
which Beverly achieves, as the dream empowers Beverly
with the knowledge of her inner strength to raise and elevate
and overcome.

11

Freedom Dreams

Freedom dreams are often dreamt by people in restrictive marriages as a form of wish-fulfillment; they hide the underlying anxiety that exists before the marital relationships end in divorce. These dreams are also dreamt after the divorce is finalized, as a form of self-affirmation or self-confirmation, wherein the divorcing or divorced spouses have become reacquainted with the joys of autonomy and personal space. (These dreams reflect the demarcation of a successful adjustment to the divorce event.) Divorce can be analogized with breaking out of jail—and in marriages wherein spousal manipulation and control are prevalent issues, freedom dreams often tend to extend territories by either empowering dreamers with flying skills or with superhuman powers that allow them to cover ground quickly so that they can make up for lost time.

Freedom dreams of flying are wonderful ego boosters, as they not only empower the dreamer with Superman/Superwoman qualities but also give a sense of omnipotence. These dreams are often dreamt by divorced females who have their feet firmly planted on terra firma but would like the chance to lift up and drift aimlessly as birds. The act of flying also manifests the wish to lighten up—enlighten—by shedding the heaviness of the divorce situation which frequently leaves female divorcées burdened with worries, particularly of the financial kind. (Flying dreams of male divorcés are often attached to sexual excitation because inherent in the act of flying is that which rises up against the pull of gravity.)

Freedom dreams express the need for personal freedom, independence, and autonomy, and reflect the dreamer's new sense of self-direction. With control of their lives again in the hands of the divorced spouses, freedom of choice is often a dream motif. Regarding choice, the divorced focus extends beyond the narrow parameters of the marital focus.

Frequently the culmination of a bad marriage is revisualized in dreams as a definite end point that serves to remind dreamers of their new beginnings—they gaze in wonder at an independent self, at an individual and sole presence. Further along as the attachment to an ex-spouse dwindles, a separate identity reemerges and can do whatever it chooses.

One year later, precisely at the moment when her divorce had become final the following freedom dream was dreamt by my literary agent and attorney, **Liz Berney:**

> *I am meeting with a guy in the city somewhere. He goes with me to a train station and we part ways . . . we veer in different directions. I'm running through this tunnel going really fast, speeding, but I'm not getting tired at all. I could keep running and not get tired. . . . I feel strong. This guy happens along on a motorcycle. He is a stranger who reminds me of a lifeguard who was working at a summer camp where I had worked once. I got on the back of the motorcycle . . . wordless . . . he's driving through the tunnel, he turns around and he's kissing me on the motorcycle. . . . We get out of the tunnel and I walk off sort of dismissive to him.*

After a brutal but much wished-for divorce, one's dream often repeats the moment of finalization in order to confirm to the dreamer that closure has indeed been established; this reassures the dreamer that a new beginning is taking wing. As a train station symbolizes departures and life's journeys, the guy Liz parts ways with is most likely her ex-spouse, as they veer in different directions. (The word *veer* implies a strong and definite change of course or direction and emphasizes the sense of averting or moving away from disaster.) The use of the word *guy* objectifies her ex-spouse and reflects her sense of estrangement from him.

Most appropriately Liz (and not the train) is running through the tunnel, as she is on track again with the strength, determination, and will of a locomotive. She is speeding to make up for all the lost time unhappily spent during her marital relationship. She is tireless in her efforts to get out of the tunnel—the dismal shadow of her old life. (Emerging from the tunnel—a womb symbol—represents rebirth but also emphasizes that the dreamer is leaving the restrictive existence of her spousal relationship for the light at the other end of the tunnel.)

A new man enters the scene on a motorcycle, and although a stranger, he is perceived as a lifeguard who will drive Liz out of the tunnel. The lifeguard complements the rebirth motif as he is there to assist, to pull her out of the water/amniotic fluid of the womb. His accompaniment proves beneficial as he is equipped with wheels. The stranger is the newfound masculine side of Liz's personality. The action of the word *drive* refers to the ambition and willfulness of the dreamer as she mounts the motorcycle and bonds with the masculine icon of strength and power. She is astride the motorcycle, effortlessly in full control of the situation. She is wordless because there is no one else to speak with but herself. She is giving herself the proverbial pat on the back of approval; she is kissed (stroked).

In another view, the guy who silently rides her out of the tunnel—who does her bidding—is a metaphor for how to use men to get where you want in life. Once out of the tunnel—fully empowered, fully confident—she dismisses what she no longer needs. She can go anywhere she wants with whomever she wants in a come-what-may fashion because she has found what it means to be a free agent.

The following freedom dream was dreamt by a Manhattan investor and financier, **Steve,** just before his divorce was to become final:

I was standing around with some of the guys when I tried to fly. I told them I could and they all laughed. I stood still and moved my arms up and down and nothing happened, but being determined I tried again, this time with my eyes closed, and suddenly I felt myself lifting off the ground. When I opened my eyes I was already over the heads of my friends, who were amazed at my skill. I looked down at them and said, "See ya, you can't have lunch with me today because I am wanted in Paris."

Steve's flying is certainly a confirmation of his will to succeed on his own (he can fly without wings or an airplane); however, the validity of this fact must be rather tenuous as his flying has to be witnessed—thus he is watched by friends, as he is eager for self-esteem. In his ability to fly and rise above his friends he has outclassed them. Interesting. Steve is only able to fly with his eyes closed—what better metaphor for denial! Steve is shutting off some sobering reality he does not choose to see or recognize, a reality nonpermissive of light-hearted tomfoolery or inappropriate, irresponsible behavior that would keep him if not sullen certainly serious and most definitely grounded (most probably the heaviness of his pending divorce).

Looking down at his friends is metaphorically condescending, in that by lowering or degrading his friends he is elevating himself in status. The dream depicts Steve as too importantly busy to lunch with his friends, as Paris is waiting (Paris, as a city that can be entered, is sexualized as a woman). Steve has a rendezvous with a beautiful, exciting, and glamorous woman. The fact that he is wanted in Paris highlights his male desirability. The friends cannot follow him to Paris or join him in his exploits. Unlike them, he is divorced and as such a free agent who can go wherever he wants whenever he wants. Quite literally, he can fly off at a moment's notice.

The following freedom dream was dreamt by the author **Jennifer Belle** after the breakup of her longtime relationship with her boyfriend. The excerpt from her diary reads:

> I had the most wonderful dream of my life last night. Around a conference table, the head of a company, a tall, good-looking man, singles me out. I take the elevator to the sixtieth floor to see him. The elevator turns over on its side and a seat belt comes down from the ceiling. I am scared but excited and I keep going. The elevator moves freely in all directions, up out of the building and into the sky. It takes me past the Empire State Building. (When I left the house this morning and saw the Empire State Building I felt like it was my best friend.)

Taking the elevator to the sixtieth floor symbolizes the dreamer's emotional ascent and sense of upward mobility—

continuing beyond signifies the wish to break boundaries. Similarly, when the elevator turns over on its side, it indicates a major change of direction. Moving freely in all directions represents Jennifer's newfound freedom, which is perceived as a little scary and is why a seat belt comes down from the ceiling—Jennifer wants her freedom but wants some restraints as well.

In a moment of transcendence, the elevator goes beyond the building (the material self) and into the sky—the realm of the spiritual. It goes past or supersedes the Empire State Building, the phallic representation of male superiority. She has been singled out by the head of the company and, as top man, has her own phallus and is not in need of another, at least momentarily!

The dream is perceived as most wonderful because in taking the elevator the dreamer is elevating her view of life. The tall, good-looking man is the Empire State Building (possibly her ex-beau) who she is over and past, which is why, in the morning, the building is viewed as her best friend.

12

Survival Dreams

Survival dreams are statements of accomplishment. They are self-affirmations that dispel the threatening idea of being a victim. Survival dreams are all about keeping oneself from harm through the arrangement of protective measures. A dream of this sort is meant to banish any feeling of insecurity or uncertainty of outcome.

As Darwin has put it, the nature of life, of humans, of all things living is geared toward survival. The will to survive is not only a matter of technique but also an involuntary wired-in reflex. Survival dreams are dreamt as sureties, confirmations that one will make it on one's own. To survive from a catastrophic event such as a divorce, which can pull the emotional rug out from under one's stoical feet, is difficult and all the more reason for one to rely on intuition and belief in oneself. This kind of recognition often manifests itself in dreams of survival.

When the self loses its significant other, the principal motive for keeping oneself from drowning in an abyss of self-pity is survival. As every action is viewed as a measure of will, survival dreams are chock full of actions in which the dreamer is perceived as having decision-making control. These dreams reinforce the dreamer's lagging internal perception of his or her own sense of strength, endurance, and autonomy, and the ability to initiate.

Although survival dreams are often founded on a conscious perception of weakness and neediness, the dreams therapeutically expose the opposite view in a directed effort to stabilize a floundering sense of self. Unaided by outside or external help, these dreams allow their dreamers to tap into their own inner strength, fortitude, determination, and will. Survival dreams warn dreamers that they have had a close call—Phew! . . . and that a similar situation could arise again. These dreams reveal how important it is to be wary and prepared and to trust one's better instincts.

The following survival dream was dreamt by **Robert Mosbacher,** former secretary of commerce, twice Olympic-class world sailing champion, and CEO of Mosbacher Energy Company, during his divorce proceedings:

I'm in a boat in a terrible storm, not sure I'm going to make it but I'm sailing through it to an island I never knew existed, with a beautiful white beach, aqua water, and palm trees. I anchor the boat, having been concerned with survival, and feel the peace and contentment you feel on a boat when things have gone well.

Robert's boat ride through the storm is viewed as a substitutive act. As a boat represents the structure or foundation of life, riding the boat through a storm symbolizes a stressful, rocky time when Mr. Mosbacher is being jostled about, his foundations shaken (divorce is on the horizon). The troubled waters are the difficulties of coming to terms with divorce, and although he is intimately associated with the impulse to turn back, he weathers the storm. The terrible storm threatens to alter the dreamer's course of action, or, at the very least, throw him off course. But, whereas the storm should prevent moving ahead, the dreamer's perseverance drives him forward—as progression is desired.

Thus, (even without muse, wife Georgette) the dreamer sails through rough waters to a place that he never knew existed or felt capable of reaching. He anchors his boat in an effort to reestablish stability—the island he anchors at represents the independent and autonomous male ego (the land of "I"), but more important symbolizes self-discovery. The discovery of the island (an inner sanctity) enables the dreamer to rid himself of doubt—the security of his mental life and manhood is assured. For after all, Mosbacher is no longer at sea, but alongside terra firma (solid ground).

The dreamer has exceeded his own expectations. Where other men may have turned back, capitulated, or capsized Robert has gone the distance, met the challenge, and reached the shores of contentment intact and at peace, for having survived is the self-realization that activates peace of mind.

The following is an example of a negative survival dream, wherein the enterprise of survival is based on the demise of another, and wherein a personal confirmation is achieved at the expense, detriment, demoralization, or minimization of another. The dream belongs to **Mr. B.,** an ex-husband of a former patient (Alice). He relayed his dream to Alice while he was still her fiancé. The day before the dream Alice had asked her fiancé, Mr. B., to assist her in moving from her apartment. He had helped her load up shopping carts with objects from her home. This was the day residue of the dream that Mr. B. (now Alice's ex-husband) hastened to tell Alice, as he claimed that this dream was what convinced him of his love for her. His dream is as follows:

I dreamt that you were in a shopping cart and that you were blind and I was pushing you around.

The symbol of the shopping cart is twofold: it suggests a constrictive cage and at the same time objectifies the fiancée into an item pulled from a shelf. Being blind further diminishes the autonomy of the fiancée, who is viewed as helpless, dependent, and in need of guidance and direction. She cannot see and therefore has no insight into the situation (the cramped space) she has gotten herself into.

The wheels of the cart indicate the immobility of her legs—her entrapment. The dreamer (the husband to be, and future ex-spouse) is the one in control—the one who is doing the steering—the one who is pushing Alice around, which seems Mr. B.'s actual wish—to push his fiancée around. The dream self-empowers the dreamer at the expense of someone else's ability to fend for themselves.

In reality, time would indeed prove the dreamer (as husband) an extremely controlling and manipulative individual—one who became both verbally and physically abusive. Had Alice interpreted her fiancé's dream correctly she would never have married him and would have avoided the difficult and painful experience of a divorce.

The following survival dream was dreamt by **Carolyne Roehm** sometime after her divorce:

> *I walk over this hill and look down into a low valley. I walked down into it where there is this glorious glowing blue light. There is the serenity of a nativity scene . . . white colors, blue colors. I think how beautiful all this color is.*

Whereas walking up a hill represents the arduous path to the top, walking over the hill means that the dreamer has already been there—already traveled the road to personal achievement and fame—and has gone beyond. Walking over this hill suggests an obstacle or impediment en route that has already been surmounted and most certainly alludes to the divorce event, which is often perceived as a personal low in one's life—a bottoming out. Yet, in Carolyne's world there is no place for the structure of weakness, which is why there is no structure standing, but only colored light. (There is no longer anything material, or superficial, as this has been seen to dissipate.) What is viewed most respectfully, however, is immaterial and thus lasting.

Looking down into a low valley represents the yearning for depth, understanding, and discovery. As the valley is the vast unconscious, entering the valley is the wish to reach the instinctive foundations and see where the root of self-recognition grows. By walking into the blue light Carolyne is bravely and figuratively walking into the blue (unprotected by her ex-spouse), into the unknown, mysterious regions that require faith and intuition. Carolyne's impulse of love has displaced itself onto the environment, and a sense of isolation is transformed by a glowing light. The light becomes hospitable—an endearing presence.

The dream is dreamt as a compensation for the self-doubt produced by the divorce event and as an adjustment for an inner void or isolation, which is why it occurs in a hallowed glowing spot that has the serenity of a nativity scene, the sense of inspirational renewal and rebirth. Carolyne's survival dream is filled with utopian hope, as something is brightening and awakening within her unconscious. Thus, she sees the light. As one must look below the surface to find one's true colors, the dream is a wish for truth. The color blue—true blue—represents sincerity. The glowing blue light reflects spiritual contentment and is self-revelatory. Carolyne has the realization how beautiful all this is, in a manner that suggests she has come to terms with her divorce. Carolyne's survival dream has encountered self-containment, a by-product of independence and a meaningful reconstruction of her marital disruption.

13

Dreams of Loss or Losing Things

Loss dreams reflect the overestimation in our psyche of things material but also reflect the emotional value placed on marital objects given up during a divorce. Houses, as we already know, are representations of the personality and as such are somatic investments (see Redecorating and Refurbishing the Home: The Female Imago). In that marital houses represent a shared spousal intimacy, they transcend thoughts of destructibility and impermanence in a way that is consistent with the instinct of self-preservation. The marital home therefore lends the spouse a future to the extent that the spouse is linked to the home and anchored to its spousal existence.

As houses symbolize our emotional environments and sanctity, losing a marital house has great significance, as we become disenfranchised from that part of our self that was linked to a marital partner. The marital home is usually viewed as an abstraction of the spousal buyer (the one who owns the home), which makes losing the home (through divorce) perceived as the loss of a loved one.

As loss is symbolic of detachment, a divorce always gives the sense of something being taken away—a slice withdrawn from a pie that is irrecoverable and oftentimes produces a melancholia for the object lost (in that we always want what we cannot have) and for the self, which has a fear of becoming impoverished.

In that memories are retrieved by their association with persons, times, and places, there are parts of us that relate to specific persons so that a separation from them diminishes us in some way. As any loss permeates the sense of self, it is either associated with injustice or on the other end of the scale self-critical reproaches that necessarily refer to a diminution of self-esteem as seen through objects wherein the objects are viewed as extensions of ourselves and self-worth.

Dreaming of something lost is reflective of need or desire, as desire refers to that which is missing. Loss can bring about the sense of emptiness, but it can also necessarily produce a feeling of lack, or powerlessness at not having prevented the loss from occurring. As acquisition rises out of a need for being nurtured by the external world, any loss is perceived as a hunger that must be gratified. Thus dependence is placed on objects as they extend and solidify the individual. (A house can give the sense of fullness to a void within the individual.)

When things are taken away from an individual, control issues often follow. Usually one knows whom they have lost but sometimes not explicitly what they have lost or how in fact they have lost it until it is too late. Whether the loss be an object (car or house) or ex-spouse, the loss belongs to the ego. Metaphorically, dreaming of an object lost expresses the need to fill the emotional void of its absence. Dreams of loss (particularly in regard to divorce) can often point to an ambivalence or wistfulness (even conflict) over the marital dissolution. Finally, if love cannot be given up it takes refuge in narcissistic identification with the object's substitute.

The following loss dream was dreamt by the author and beautiful supermodel **Carmen** the year following her divorce:

I dreamt of being outside my former house and wanting to go inside and clean things up. I was annoyed that I had no control over what was going on inside the house, or of who was in the house . . . of what people they were entertaining. I would not have had them. Neighbors were very solicitous—inviting me in for tea.

Losing a marital house means that one can no longer enter the door of the marital world of control and stability, as it no longer belongs to one. Similarly, being outside a former house represents a certain self-estrangement and reveals the desire to go back inside, to be welcomed back into the fold of familiarity.

The wish to clean things up is reparative in nature and can only mean that the dreamer wants to put her life back in order and to regain a measure of control that was lost during the divorce event. With control lost, the house is messy, as there is no order. But the act of cleaning up may also reflect the dreamer's desire to replace things as they were—to remarry!

Having no control over what was going on inside the house depicts the dreamer on the sidelines of a lifestyle that she has lost. Yet, there is the realization that the dreamer would not have (like her ex-spouse) entertained certain people (or ideas), which suggests that Carmen is different from her ex-spouse.

Neighbors become wishful substitutes for her ex-spouse, as they are dreamt of as solicitous and understanding. Inviting Carmen into their homes for tea allows Carmen to remain near her home—to drink and be nurtured in the proximity of her old home (albeit, she has to swallow the situation)—and preserve a sense of self-righteousness and acceptance.

The following dream of loss was dreamt by **Alice** during her divorce proceedings and is as follows:

I was in Central Park, inside a small circle of friends holding hands. I had to leave for a phone call. When I came back they said there was no longer any room for me. I ran over to the other end of the park. I was riding on the merry-go-round hoping to grab one of the golden rings but I kept missing it.

As a circle is the symbol of wholeness and unity, it is most appropriate that it is used to symbolize the marital union in the form of a ring. Being enclosed inside a small circle establishes the feeling of security and belonging that the dreamer feels as a married spouse. The holding of the hands represents the bond of matrimony. Being shunned from that circle expresses the dreamer's sense of self-estrangement and role confusion—there is no longer any room for her.

With the circle lost to her (there is no more incorporation in the group), the dreamer runs toward a substitute, another kind of circle, a "merry-go round" that in a regressive sense brings her "round" again in the sought after merry mood of youth. But circling the object of her desire is not enough—she is after the golden ring that has been lost via the divorce. The fact that she keeps missing it reveals how much Alice regrets the dissolution of her marriage and the sense of wholeness it conveyed.

14

Looking Back / Assessment Dreams / Dreams of Responsibility

D reams of falling, although characterized by underlying anxiety, in that one visualizes oneself plummeting to the depths, often represent a surrender to a current stressful situation (falling into the error of one's ways). What looking back/assessment dreams/responsibility dreams have in common is that they are all concerned with past relationships that have changed over the years at a time when the dreamers (being more distanced/disengaged from their divorces) have a detachment that enables them an objective view, a view unblemished by any prior justifications, intellectual or emotional.

In that changes take place over time, a reevaluation of what happened and its significance is possible. As these dreams refer to marital relationships that ended in divorce, they act as an evaluative process that sometimes is able to determine why a divorce happened (see Philippe Junot). These dreams of assessment are never far from confronting one's sense of personal responsibility (see Sheila Ryan). Regarding divorce, these dreams reveal the ex-spouse's unconscious understanding of the event and thus, as a by-product, the emotions this understanding engendered. Sometimes these dreams recall broken relationships in order to facilitate emotional expression (see Laura Hunt).

☽

The following looking back/assessment dream was dreamt by the bon vivant **Philippe Junot** many years after his much publicized divorce from Princess Caroline of Monaco:

I dreamt I was obliged to drive a Formula One in the Monaco Grand Prix. I made all effort not to look ridiculous (because of former ties, my old family relationship with Monaco). It was very hard. Cars on each side of me. Making turns with my head outside from the centrifugal force.

This is a dream about living life in the fast lane, where the road ahead is always full of turns—where high performance is expected. The cars on each side represent Philippe feeling hemmed in, his skills tested. His head is outside for some breathing space. The centrifugal force means the pressure is on. (It should be noted that the more public a commitment is, the more threatening it is to have it challenged. Similarly, such perceived threat of social criticism can diminish self-esteem and necessitate defensive actions, such as infidelity, in the service of the male ego.)

Philippe's dream can be viewed as a metaphor for his former familial relationship with Princess Caroline and the Grimaldi family, where he felt obliged to show drive and ambition. The Formula One is a lone rider with a powerful engine; it symbolizes the daring nature of the dreamer, perhaps what endeared him to Monaco's grand prize—Princess Caroline. Within the assessment dream Philippe assures himself that an effort was made, but it was very hard maintaining a relationship as there were spectators everywhere!

Philippe's phrase "It was very hard" reexamines and re-confirms his sexuality and more specifically his virility, yet also refers to the excitement and difficulty of the chase—to cross the finish line first (performance anxiety) and curry favor.

The following dream of responsibility was dreamt by socialite **Laura Hunt** several years after her divorce:

> *I was driving in my car and there was this large pelican*
> *flying that crashed into the front of my car and I looked*
> *at his face and was shocked to see the sweet face of an*
> *old man. I was sobbing. I felt overwhelmed by sorrow.*

The driver of a car is the one in charge of the situation—the responsible one—as the wheel of life is symbolically in her hands. A head-on collision represents a meeting of the ways, the wish for connection. Crashing into someone is confrontational and means that there is a desire to make an impact, but may also reflect the wish to make someone inaccessible accessible, to make someone halt, to gain someone's attention.

The large pelican represents a scavenger who will hunt, but also conceals an obscure reference to the surname of Laura's ex. The bird symbolizes a lofty, free-spirited individual (a past relationship) who has risen above the daily restraints of existence. There was distance between the driver and the pelican that made the relationship falter. Thus, the dream is a crash course in communication that reestablishes contact—for there were words left unspoken.

There is sorrowful misperception—the dreamer is shocked to see the sweet face of an old man on a pelican's body. But recognition is reached when Laura perceives sweetness and even helplessness in someone previously perceived as being aloof and independent.

The following assessment dream was dreamt by the actress **Sheila Ryan** some years after her divorce from actor James Caan:

> *I was at some celebration but it was unhappy. There were people all around. I went to this aboveground pool. There was this fish in the pool, made of flesh. Someone had poured salt in the pool and the fish was being poisoned. We tried to flush the water out but the fish died. There was a dog with its paws on the pool edge. I said, "Good-bye, puppy fish." I was crying.*

Sheila Ryan dreamt an intuitive dream filled with sad recognition. The pool represents her body with its internal fluids; the water inside the pool signifies amniotic fluid as there is a fetus swimming within—a fish made of flesh. The aboveground pool is the bulging stomach of the pregnancy, the salt in the pool reminiscent of the saline-type solution used to induce abortions. To flush something out refers to an abortion. The abortion is the unhappy event, as there is a funeral. The puppy symbolizes the baby to whom the dreamer has tearfully said good-bye. The puppy fish is the offspring of the dog. Thus, the dog is the father of the baby, the apathetic onlooker.

In another view, the dream is a metaphor for a failed relationship that literally aborted—as one says good-bye to a married lifestyle that goes down the tubes or literally drowns. The salt poured into the water symbolizes a preservative—a measure of how Sheila tried to save her marriage. Either way, ex-husband Caan, as canine, seems to be in the doghouse.

15

Falling or
Falling-Apart Dreams

D reams of falling, although characterized by an underlying anxiety in that one visualizes oneself plummeting to the depths, often represent a surrender to a current stressful situation (falling into the error of one's ways). One could say that falling dreams occur during a divorce because one is no longer on familiar ground, but also because falling represents being unsupported or independent—one falls because there is no longer any symbolic (spousal) attachment to hold on to. The falling is echoic, as the falling expresses a continuity of movement in tandem with the dissolution of the marital union falling apart, wherein one's balance has been upset.

The nature of falling dreams is to establish trust in oneself that one will survive, as one never usually hits the ground or hits bottom. These dreams also require that one let go and lean back into the thin air of existence to allow oneself to be caught by the enormous callused hands of faith. Falling dreams also reflect the instability of the moment and reveal a loss of control. The underlying anxiety is generally produced by surrendering to one's impulses regardless of the consequences.

Yet, falling dreams dreamt during the breakup of a marital relationship often take on a metaphorical situation-specific meaning: divorce is associated with the fall of humans from grace.

During her divorce proceedings **Marcy,** president and CEO of Azure, an Internet website, dreamt the following two falling motif dreams. The first is as follows:

> *I am falling off an enormous mountain. I am falling in the air but I never hit the ground. Then the scene changes to a peaceful green meadow, where I lay down and sleep.*

Generally speaking, dreams of falling represent anxiety over a loss of control and a loss of balance. Indeed, there is a certain edginess involved in falling off a mountain. A sense of gravity is pulling the dreamer downward. The divorce is the gravity of the situation, which pulls on the unconscious. Falling off an enormous mountain means that there is no more ground underneath, no more structure to hold on to. We are reminded of the line from Yeats's "The Second Coming," which reads, "the center cannot hold," and refers to an anticipated collapse of society as we know it, wherein things will fall apart and an anarchy will reign supreme.

The mountain is viewed as a massive physical presence and indicates that Marcy associates her divorcing spouse with great strength and power. Leaving the spouse is therefore perceived as a threatening situation in which Marcy no longer feels either protected or secure in her environment. Yet, the innate pluckiness of the dreamer is established, as she never hits the ground, she never hits bottom. The change of scene is the wish for just that—an environmental or situational change for the better. Finding oneself in a peaceful green meadow is the wish to escape from stress; releasing the tension of the moment will enable relaxation and even sleep. Thus, the dreamer, comfortable in her newfound environment, reveals that in some way she has mentally adapted to the necessary fall she has had to take in order for her to enjoy a peaceful sleep. The color green is associated with virginity and purity and is therefore interpreted as a wish for rebirth, to start anew.

Marcy's second frequently recurring falling dream is as follows:

I am falling from an airplane but I never break into a million pieces because I land in water.

This falling dream contains the same falling symbolism, the falling from great heights to great depths, yet once again the dreamer's fall does not necessitate that she hit bottom or break into a million pieces—her fall is broken as she very positively and optimistically lands in water. The fear that the dreamer is working through is the fear of falling to pieces, which she does not do and will not do. The water (as with the color green in the first dream) also symbolizes birth. Thus, to be in water is once more the wish for rebirth. As water also represents the unconscious, Marcy is in touch with her innermost feelings, which is why she is able to stay afloat and survive the trauma of divorce. The plane is a symbol that is also phonetically rendered as plain. Marcy falls from the plain because things are no longer simple.

Falling-apart dreams are visually reactive to the internal physical sense of dissolution and destruction caused by the divorce, whereby the splitting of the marital couple is felt as a rupturing or deconstructing experience. These dreams often produce symbolically significant images of shattering glass, broken china, or crumbling edifices.

The following falling-apart dream was dreamt by **Lorinda** during her lengthy divorce proceedings:

I saw two buildings and an exterior walkway (structural overpass) between the two. Suddenly the walkway broke in two and collapsed to the ground, bringing the two buildings with it.

The two buildings are perceived as the dreamer and her new lover as the couple are separated by her soon-to-be ex-husband who is still in the picture in the form of an impediment—a structural overpass between the two. When the exterior walkway collapses, most interestingly, instead of growing closer (with no further obstruction between them) the couple falls apart as well, this implies that the husband is holding together the new affair.

The dreamer's insecurity, brought on by the divorce, depicts her new relationship falling apart or collapsing, as she unconsciously believes that her inaccessibility is precisely what has drawn her lover to her in the first place. Ironically, the success and durability of her new relationship proves to be based on the existence of her divorcing husband—on his perceived powerful presence.

Thus, the dream reveals Lorinda's sense of dependence on her marital structure and her need for continuance of a lifestyle symbolized by spousal stability.

16

Dreams of Not Being Able to Move or Speak

Dreams of not being able to move or speak are quite common, as they usually occur at a time when the dreamer is in conflict about a life situation in which a decision must be reached, a choice be made. Being in conflict literally means not knowing which way to turn, which is why this type of dream often has the paralyzing effect of creating stasis (conflict is not usually permissive of aggressive action either in one direction or the other).

These dreams reflect that the dreamer is having a difficult time getting from point A to point B as he or she is held in a holding pattern of indecisiveness—the dreamers are usually sitting on the fence (or should I say stuck on the fence) betwixt and between. These semiparalytic dreams speak volumes (albeit sometimes silently) about responsibility, as responsibility demands that one get up and move and initiate an action. Most important, dreams of this nature mean that one is biding one's time.

When a marriage is breaking down and divorce is contemplated the thinking process goes into overload, as one is beset by emotional, financial, social, and familial worries, not to mention a troubled conscience. Yet, by being immobile the dreamer is buying time.

The most telling aspect of these dreams is the intentionality of a near motionless state.

The following recurrent nonmoving dream was dreamt by the male supermodel **Cameron** during the dissolution of his marital relationship:

There are some people chasing me but I can never seem to run very fast or run away from things or people. It suddenly all becomes slow motion when I try to run, as though I were underwater.

Even a simple dream like this one is a complex way of looking at things. As an anxiety dream, and in a sense a dream of inhibition, the dream reveals motives of resistance or reluctance on the part of the dreamer. The dream is involved with the conflict between movement and stasis where an unresolved choice can render one motionless. The dreamer may, in fact, seek this powerless condition that forestalls any decision making (the decision to divorce); in simpler terms, the dreamer may not be able to (or know how to) say no. (Restrictions are placed by individuals on themselves as a measure of precaution for the purpose of protection.)

In that the dreamer wants to run but is being thwarted by his own body, by the unwillingness of his own legs to move effortlessly, one must assume that there is good reason, that there is intentionality behind this. (Many dreamers, like Cameron, have reported having felt the heaviness and futility of trying to move quickly through waist-high water.) Thus, as the decision to move is not operational, the dream reveals the classic fear of loss of control. This may suggest that the dreamer feels that he is not controlling his life decisions or that the decisions he has made are not being followed through to fruition.

Additionally, not running fast enough signifies that there is not enough time. Perhaps demands are being made that the dreamer is unprepared to accede to. In actuality, the desire may be to flee, but out of an innate sense of obligation and responsibility the dreamer is unable to do so. He instead becomes motionless or moves slowly as if he is in slow motion. Yet this movement that is perceived as being in slow motion is at the specific request of the dreamer; in other words, the dreamer wishes to have more time to evaluate the situation at hand (in this case, his marital relationship) almost in freeze frame.

The dreamer needs time to assimilate all the details and weigh the options available to him; this reflects his thoughtful, conscientious, and nonimpulsive nature. Interestingly, the dreamer desires to keep at bay not only people but things that he cannot run away from. These things may be interpreted as situations or decisions or responsibilities. The lack or difficulty of moving often reflects a desire to tread softly in life, not to violate, trespass, or evoke anger.

Another dream in which movement (particularly movement forward) was restricted is one wherein the dreamer was trying hard to move forward, and it was imperative to do so, because he was being chased. But as hard as he tried to progress, he simply could not move ahead and was forced to remain stationary for the remainder of the dream, as though his body had turned into the trunk of a tree.

The dream belongs to **Jerry,** a radio call-in who told me his dream over the nationally syndicated *Victoria Jones Show.* His dream is as follows:

I am outside in a field. I am being chased (I do not know by whom, and I do not look back to find out!). I cannot really run . . . the harder I try the more slow I become. I am running away from something but I am not able to run from it.

In actuality, although Jerry did not really want to proceed farther along, he certainly did not want to look back in the direction that his current life was headed, as he had just gotten separated from his wife and was contemplating getting a swift divorce. Through the process of denial he had evidentially and symbolically placed behind him the very situation that had made him anxious (hence, he does not look behind him in the dream to see what he is running from).

To say he is running from something is itself an admission that he is not facing his responsibilities, as he is being chased from behind. Being outside in a field symbolizes his new-found freedom and also expresses that perhaps he would like to play the field, as he is lingering there. But what is most important is the intentionality of the inaction—Jerry does not run but is rather prevented from doing so.

The couple had not gone for any marital counseling and had come to a somewhat abrupt decision to separate. Yet by discussing his dream Jerry was able to recognize that he was unable to decide the correct course of action—he felt that he may have been rushing into something that he would later regret. With this in mind it is no wonder that his dream wish was not to run, but to slow down a rapidly moving process.

In this way Jerry's dream may be viewed as protective in nature and necessarily successful at slowing down the momentum by not allowing Jerry to be carried away by the impulsive young wings of emotion. To be sure, as *chased* is phonetically rendered as *chaste* the fact that Jerry is being chased means that he is attempting to keep his moral and ethical values intact. This is most probably why he took stock of his dream in the first place.

17

Retribution Dreams

Sweet is revenge—especially to women.
BYRON, *DON JUAN*

D reams of retribution have a purgatorial quality in that
they offer dreamers a cathartic release of pent-up anger
and frustration. These dreams are enjoyed by many
dreamers who are either going through or have gone through
difficult divorces that have left them with the wish to discredit
their ex-spouses. But whereas most retribution cannot be
acted out due to retaliatory actions, the dreamworld achieves
them unconsciously.

Retribution dreams are dreams of getting even that perfectly mete out the punishment that fits the crime (see Andrea
Reynolds, Marilyn Sokol). The dreams represent payback
time in the privacy of one's home and are viewed as expres-
sions of hostility directed outward in a socially acceptable
manner. Sometimes the dreams exteriorize the dreamer's
anger in the form of parable, which has at its root a moral basis.

Shakespeare's *Hamlet* is thematically soaked in retribution, but alas, Hamlet's retaliative actions follow too slowly
and therefore bring about his demise. If only he could have
dreamt away his anger. In the movie *The War of the Roses,* a
divorcing spouse's anger finds its pleasurable outlet in acting
out negative impulses during wakefulness, yet the actions
seem wedded to the unconscious id.

Andrea Reynolds (who during the interval of her divorce

proceedings was dating Claus Von Bulow) had been in court for almost two years during which time she had had to view Sheldon Reynolds (her soon-to-be ex-spouse) representing himself. As he was immensely charming—a real bon vivant/raconteur—the trial was taken with him to the point that he was somewhat palsy-walsy with the judge. On one particular day while speaking with the judge, Andrea remembered seeing Sheldon approach the bench and lean his elbow on the judge's bench, at which point the judge softly reminded Sheldon that he had to stay where he was supposed to be—at least four feet away from the bench.

The next night, incorporating all she had witnessed, Andrea dreamt the following dream of retribution:

Sheldon was placing his elbow on the judge's bench (in a charming, casual manner), doing the same thing he had done the other day, but this time he suddenly lost his pants. They fell to his ankles in the middle of the New York Supreme Court. (In reality he wore Jockey shorts but in the dream he had no underpants.)

The wish of Andrea's retribution dream is to discredit her husband's credibility—to show or reveal him as he really is— which is why the dream literally and figuratively exposes him, as he is caught with his pants down. (The subtle insinuation is that Sheldon is an ass.) But in losing his pants, Sheldon is also stripped of his manliness, as he is no longer wearing the pants. Adding insult to injury, as Sheldon is facing the judge, he is presented to the jury and the courtroom spectators as ass backwards.

His seduction of the judge with his casual charm and ingratiating manner is exposed, as Sheldon is put in a most compromising position wherein the truth of the matter, it is hoped, will be laid bare. Wearing no underpants means the truth can be unveiled. Familiarity aside, there will be no more elbows on benches!

The pants fall all the way down to Sheldon's ankles so that his butt-naked humiliation is complete. Moreover, in order to retrieve his fallen pants he will be required to bend, an action that would grant Andrea the satisfaction she desires.

The following retribution dream was dreamt by the actress **Marilyn Sokol** some time after the breakup of a relationship that would have led to marriage if not for a certain other woman who married Marilyn's ex instead. Her dream is as follows:

> *I got up out of my bed to strangle with my own hands the woman who broke up my premarital relationship. I went into her home and into her bed and strangled her.*

Marilyn's retribution dream was a long time in coming but when it finally came it was a hands-on physical experience—she uses her own two hands to strangle her female adversary. Her dream is transparently clear like the dreams of young children that are often without the trappings of disguise—so pure and justified are their motives. By going into the marital bed of the other woman, Marilyn insinuates herself into the heart of the matter where it hurts most. In that the other woman metaphorically emptied or violated Marilyn's premarital bed by stealing her companion it is Marilyn's turn to do the same—to deprive her ex-companion of his marital spouse and leave his bed empty.

The punishment of choice certainly fits the crime as Marilyn strangles and thus suffocates the other woman. One can only imagine the feeling of being squeezed out of a love relationship by another woman and the claustrophobic, suffocating sense of having to make room for someone new.

Indeed, Marilyn's retribution dream afforded her the joyous solace she had been looking for. To Marilyn, strangling this other woman must have been breathtaking!

The following is an example of a negative retribution dream, which was dreamt by a former patient, **Alec,** as a form of self-punishment in an attempt to rid himself of a guilt founded on his sudden divorce:

I was walking down an unfamiliar street that was very dark. I heard gunshots and came across a motionless body bleeding or maybe dead on the sidewalk. I was not sure. The body was facedown so I could not see the face but I somehow felt that I knew the woman. I tried to get help by running into this office to use the telephone. As I opened the door a man shot me in the stomach.

The unfamiliar street represents to the dreamer his new address and necessarily his new marital home, the mere thought of which makes him uncomfortable enough to present as being very dark and even dangerous, as gunshots are heard and a body lies in its wake. Implicit is the idea that if the dreamer were not on that street (did not leave his wife) a body (his ex-wife) would not be found in a sorry state.

The body is facedown because Alec does not want to see the pain he has caused his ex-wife. The word *body* is mentioned twice, objectified without its gender, as Alec would like to stay as detached as possible from any recognition of the culpability of himself or his ex-wife. Yet, his guilt is at such a fever pitch that his wish remains, to be punished.

The office he runs to for some protective mediation is most

probably that of his psychoanalyst, as there is a telephone (a symbol of communication). Similarly, as he opens the door (recognizes his feelings of guilt and remorse) he is punished (shot) as a means of assuaging his guilt.

Being a heartbreaker his own heart must be broken in self-retribution which is why he is shot in an organ of nourishment, for everyone knows that the way to a man's heart is through his stomach!

18

Dreams of Recognition

Marriage is like a hedge fund that one feels scurrilous looking behind. Therefore, for many reasons, one of the most difficult realizations is coming to grips with the idea that one's marriage is not working. There is always the judgmental sense of personal failure or inadequacy. There is the sense of permanence slipping away; there is the fear of one's own mortality. There is always separation anxiety, worry over change, and the depressive sense of despair based on feelings of dependency.

But recognition dreams bare one's soul and give fresh perspective on an underexposed tucked-in-the-drawer assessment of the marital relationship. Recognition in itself plays a major role in the coping process (it is viewed as a wound that must be uncovered in order to be healed). For through recognition comes the clarification of actuality and through actuality the qualitative understanding of essence.

These dreams are introspective and based on the observation of one's repressed emotional experience within the confines of the marital relationship. With nothing screened out, these dreams acknowledge the worst, as they successfully hack through the underbrush of defensive self-deception and the reality distortion that is usually a feature in socially or emotionally determined conscious coping.

Recognition of any failed enterprise (particularly a marital one) is usually exhausting and leaves the individual longing to drink from the waters—the Greek mythological springs of Lethe—as oblivion is often the only respite from a dismal albeit partly submerged reality. But a dream of recognition (a reflection of our inner psyche) is one our unconscious has already familiarized to the extent that the dream becomes a determined correspondent with consciousness.

The following recurring recognition dreams were dreamt by supermodel **Chris Royer** before she came to terms with the fact that her marriage was over. The first is as follows:

I was with a body, a male form, but really there was no one there. I was alone. I thought I was dreaming of waking up. I wake up in the dream and find there was nothing there. The body was not the body of my husband. It looked like a duplication had occurred like in the body snatchers.

Within the dream is a disembodied description of emotion that heightens the objective quality of how a person appraises a negatively changing relationship. Being with a body or a male form already depersonalizes Chris's spouse and draws attention to his sense of absence from the marital scene and necessarily her sense of isolation and profound loneliness. There is no substance to her marital life or relationship.

The dream is a wake-up call—a nihilistic realization that there is nothing there. In that nothing can come from nothing the thought is insufferable. The dreamer wishes to wake up within the dream, as a means of escape, only to find that she has already awakened. Interestingly, there is the recognition that there is no recognition—the body is *not* the body of her husband. A duplication has occurred which gives one the sense that a profound change has taken place. The original (in as far as it relates to a philosophical ideal of the conjugal union) is nowhere to be found, as it has been metaphorically snatched away.

In a McLuhanesque sense Chris's dream makes the dismal recognition that her present marriage is one of form without content. And whereas the medium of recognition is marriage, the message is divorce!

Chris's second recurring dream of recognition contains a falling motif and is ideationally strongly related to her first. Both dreams recognize loneliness and the low expressive resonance of futility. The dream is as follows:

I'd be walking off a cliff. I'd land on solid ground but everything was darkening.

In interpreting this recurring dream of recognition, a line from Rabelais comes to mind: "I am just going to leap into the dark." What is recognized herein is a sense of dislocation and disorientation in one's life, as stability is gone. Land falls off from underfoot just as easily as land reappears. Vapors such as air solidify into solid ground. There is the sense of somnambulism—sleepwalking through one's existence.

Although walking off a cliff is deemed intentionally suicidal, landing on solid ground is the preferred afterlife as it reestablishes stability and the pragmatism of substance. Either way, the picture is darkening, which indicates a bleak state of emotional affairs that is about to darken further, as the picture symbolizes the dissolution of Chris's marriage—as literally underfoot. Yet one thing is certain, what is unknown (outside the marital relationship) is better than what is known! The recognition is that the time is ripe to take the plunge.

☽

The following dream of recognition dreamt by a former male patient is as follows:

> *I walked over to a large capital letter* I *and noticed that the two horizontal lines were hemming in the vertical line. Hard as I tried to elevate, to lift up the top horizontal slab, it wouldn't move. Then I noticed much to my surprise that a large feline cat or panther was seated on top of the structure. No matter how much food I placed at the foot of the structure the cat would have none of it and would not vacate her position.*

Within the context of this dream, the large capital letter *I* undeniably symbolizes the male ego, which is noticed as being contained, hemmed in, and even claustrophobically restricted by the horizontal lines that cross its metaphorical spine or backbone—the core of its skeletal development. The vertical or upward growth (of the male persona) is prevented mobility to a higher level. Thus there is no room for elevation. In fact, the only lifting up that occurs is the enlightenment of the dreamer as to the meaning of his dream.

The large feline cat or panther is the spousal substitute who in her dominant position appears stable, self-satisfied, and already sated, as she needs nothing (no form of nourishment, emotional or otherwise) from the dreamer's offerings. At the top of the structure the female spouse appears unwilling to relinquish her position of control.

The letter in the dream, taken in its other signified meaning, is one that should be read, for its message is clear—the male spousal inhibition presented is one that is beyond mediation and one that has already promulgated ideas of divorce within the dreamer's unconscious as he tries to break away from his horizontal imprisonment or entrapment of the conjugal bed.

This next most interesting recognition dream was dreamt by the author **Jill Hoffman,** founding editor of *Mudfish,* after the breakup of her long-term relationship:

> *Nightmare. On subway outing with Vlad. Lonely. Reading. No fun. All of a sudden I realize I am alone. Because he's hiding. He's drinking. It's pointless. He's not doing anything. I want to return him to his mother. I slap his fleshy cheek that I love. I tell him he has to go. Then a pointless discussion with some woodsman who tells me I'm entitled to half of V.'s cabin that he built— that I've never seen—and don't want.*

The sense of entitlement and division (I'm entitled to half) prevalent among failed relationships emerges within the obscurity of a phantom cabin that is neither seen nor wanted. V.'s cabin, however, is his symbolic substitute, his persona, poignant in that the dream reveals Jill's lack of want.

The insightful woodsman (Jung's spirit guide or animus, the male presence in the female psyche) reveals the existence of the intangible cabin (Vlad) but the dreamer does not want to possess what is never disclosed—Vlad's essence. Vlad hides, to the point of being anonymous, as Jill suddenly realizes that she is alone. (Phonetically rendered, *woodsman* becomes *wouldsman* or *the man who would,* and emphasizes the significance of the conditional in life. Vlad comes along with the cabin.)

The subway outing is an unconscious expression of a submerged or repressed truth. The outing is the coming clean, the admission that the relationship is literally down and out. The symbolic significance of the repetition of *pointless* is that it sustains a nihilist view—the relationship that has already peaked and declined is therefore without a point. A signified recidivist, Vlad is returned to his mother as to the womb. Yet, the one who delivers the slap on his fleshy cheek is none other than the dreamer in an effort to restore an inhalation of life apart from the primary love object of the moment—the dreamer herself.

19

Dreams of Longing

The emotional isolation and rootlessness produced by divorcing spouses frequently finds its outlet in dreams of longing. In social circles being loved assumes a powerful significance, and in that our society more often than not measures our success in life (self-esteem and personal worth) by the amount of love we receive, any perceived loss of love is interpreted as a hit against our image, our psyche, our social prestige.

The concept of physiological longing is an inherent part of the evolutionary plan to survive. In a desert environment one dreams of a longing for water. In this physiological aspect dreams of longing are tied to the eternal quest of the universe to expand. Emotional longing, however, is something else entirely.

A dream of (emotional) longing does not belong to the wish-fulfillment category of dreams but is rather viewed as a motif belonging to anxiety dreams which reflect a general societal malaise. Most important, dreams of longing express the intensity of need and are viewed as manifestations of the isolation of contemporary life. But longing exists as a strong persistent craving or desire only to the extent that it remains unfulfilled. As Freud has written, "We are so made that we can derive intense enjoyment only from a contrast and very little from a state of things." In other words, desire ends in whatever it achieves. In this way dreams of longing are like crying over spilt milk.

Human longing has value as a noble sensation in that it does not or cannot demand fulfillment of its desired object, for precisely in its moment of satiation/gratification, longing dies a paradoxical death. If longing is perceived as having any practical purpose (as it has no goal or end point) it would have to be the keeping afresh of desire and the intensity of the moment.

Certain dreams of longing are nostalgic (based on past as opposed to future longing) in that they wistfully recapture dreamers making love (or wishing to make love) to former husbands or wives in times of tranquillity and complaisance, times of loyalties and affections. Oftentimes divorced dreamers seek to alter imperfect marital experiences of the past, plucking out flaws along the way. This serves to heighten the miserable sense of what is lacking in their present existence. They are the Gatsbys of this world, gaping at the end of the dock and overvaluing (in terms of character assessment) the dismal reality of what is waiting beyond the green blinking light.

There is nothing, though, that compares to feeling loved, appreciated, and sought after. And nothing that can replace a prior harmonious marital existence. And relative deprivation will not allow one who has tasted of the fruits of bliss to settle for anything less. But on life's situational road of twists and turns, at any given moment one can fall from the heights or be raised from the depths.

Dreams of longing often occur during bad marital relationships and frequently spill over into the territorial waters of divorce when spouses are looking for something to fill an emotional void.

Sometimes we do not appreciate what we have until it is

no longer ours to possess. Sometimes we undervalue our spouse's assets (emotional and physical) and find ourselves missing what we had been glad to rid ourselves of. As gain is always more well received than loss, seeing an ex-spouse with someone new may set off feelings of jealousy and remorse. Therefore a dream of longing may begin well but then take a turn for the worse leaving the dreamer angst-ridden and unfulfilled.

The following double-sided dream starts out as a dream of longing and turns into a dream of recognition. **P. M.**'s dream is as follows:

> *I had sex with my wife (whom I am currently divorcing) and then right after that I was thinking what the heck did I do as she turned into this crazy person. First she was attractive, then monstrous and out-of-control.*

It is necessary to reveal the context of P. M.'s day residue as it explains in part his wish to reclaim his ex-wife, if only briefly. The night before his dream he had seen his ex-wife at a bar with another man; this triggered thoughts of jealousy and ownership, gain and loss. The longing is for that which he can no longer have.

The recognition is that his ex-wife turned on him both in reality and in the dream. The dream reminds the dreamer that appearances can be misleading and aligns itself with P. M.'s initial perception that his wife was incompatible with him.

The love encounter in the dream is of poor quality and is thus the image that justifies the dreamer's divorce. Within the text of the dream, P. M. is able to reason, "what the heck did I do," which reaffirms his decision-making abilities. His self-image is seen as diametrically opposed to his ex-wife, as she is viewed as being out-of-control.

The dreamer is clearly in control of the situation, as he is the one who makes the critical assessment—his ex-wife's bad traits far outweigh her sexual desirability. Dreaming of being in bed with his former wife, however, may suggest that on some level he has a need to repeat the same pattern of relationship (the wrong involvement) in order to learn or resolve the nature of his need or conflict.

The following dream of longing was dreamt by **Patricia** during her marital breakup:

> *I was shopping for clothing in a store that seemed part of a huge mall. I was loaded down carrying many shopping bags. I ran into a friend of mine (who I know in reality) who was with her husband. She showed me a very expensive diamond necklace her husband had just bought her. I was admiring the necklace when suddenly my eyes became blurry. I said that my contact lens must have popped out (I don't wear them in reality) and bending down on my hands and knees pretended to look for something I knew never existed.*

Shopping alone for clothing reveals the loneliness of the dreamer and her wish to fill a void in her life. (The desire to purchase rises out of an intrapsychic need for nurturing from the external world.) Shopping in a mall makes one painfully aware of one's insignificance. Being loaded down indicates feeling weighted down and represents a heaviness in mental outlook.

The couple Patricia meets represent the longed for conjugal ideal; her girlfriend's husband represents the ultimate spousal ideal: a generous man of extravagant tastes who complacently shops *with* his wife and presents her with diamond necklaces. Not wanting to recognize her longing, Patricia's eyes become blurry (blurriness can indirectly suggest that there were tears of self-pity).

The revelation of the dream follows when Patricia pretends to look for something she knew never existed, as herein lies the real element of longing. What is most longed for in the dreamer's life is the imagined contact (both physical and emotional) that has to be made up in the dream—for even in its fictional state, it is still missing both in the text of the dream and in her marriage.

The following two longing dreams were dreamt by **L. M.**, a secretary to the vice principal of a high school, during her divorce proceedings.

I was with my ex-to-be at a resort. We were ready to go into a hotel room to have sex. I go into this room and as I go in I wake up sweating and breathing heavily and I was upset that it didn't happen.

Going into a room with one's soon-to-be ex expresses the wish to incorporate him back into the dreamer's life, as the room is a representation of herself and her world. Getting him back into bed is the desire to reestablish the marital union. Even L. M.'s unconscious is aware of the sad realization that this is a last-ditch attempt—a last resort of hers to recouple through sex, which is why she wakes up sweating and upset that it didn't happen.

In that the dream is nonpermissive of sexual intercourse, it reveals an element of conflict: the dreamer may or may not want her husband sexually. One senses that L. M. goes into the room alone in an attempt to go it alone, to be independent, a frightening prospect. Thus, upon awakening the dreamer breathes heavily.

L. M.'s next dream of longing was dreamt during a time when her house was falling apart and needed a lot of work. During this time of need L. M.'s divorcing spouse had offered his services and was acting in an extremely kind and helpful manner (almost as if guilt had set in), which is not surprising in that L. M.'s divorcing spouse had left her for a younger woman. The dream is as follows:

> *I was talking with my ex-spouse and I suggested, "Let's have sex." My ex-spouse looked at me and said, "No, it's not right."*

Bearing in mind that houses refer to the individual self, the house that in reality needs repair is seen as a representative of L. M.'s inner turmoil and state of disrepair (as caused by the divorce proceedings). To this extent, any help (either physical or economical) from the divorcing spouse is interpreted and misconstrued by the psyche as being a manifestation of the continuance of his love for her, which is why within the dream she suggests, "Let's have sex."

Although, consciously, denial is at work in the dream, the spouse's refusal validates that at least on an unconscious level the dreamer knows that her relationship is over, because it is no longer deemed as being right.

Yet, within the dream there is an element of duplicity wherein L. M. may have substituted the other woman for herself (asking for the sex) in order that the other woman (in wish-fulfillment) be rebuffed by the righteous man she would hope her spouse to be. For, in actuality, the philandering husband would never utter the words *It isn't right* without being self-condemning.

The following dream of longing was dreamt by the author **Jennifer Belle** just before the breakup of a long relationship:

*We are kissing each other through a cluster of plasticine
bubbles. I can see his lips but I am kissing the bubble.*

The longing is for the passionate fullness of a physical relationship, wherein the lips become a symbolic synecdoche—
the kissing part is overvalued as being representative of the
whole person. Yet the communion of lips is not permitted, as
there is no longer direct contact particularly in the area of
feelings.

The cluster of plasticine bubbles symbolizes protection
from breakage—bubble wraps the fragile love relationship.
The bubble is what can burst, as it signifies something insub-
stantial or ephemeral (the froth on the café latte)! In that the
bubble is transparent, Jennifer can see through the mythic romantic ideal just before it pops.

Yet, the plasticine bubbles also represent the private con-
stellations of another's identity—the worlds within worlds of
what you cannot know in someone else.

20

Rescue Fantasy Dreams

The rescue fantasy dream moves beyond an impotent marital relationship and looks outward for assistance; it often reflects the dreamer's relentless search for a way out of an oppressive situation. The dreams express the illusion of an attainable goal, whether it be a new beginning or a renewal of spirit, by juggling moral fidelities with burgeoning sexual drives and sensibilities. But as these dreams of salvation seek outside help they are based on dependency, depicting dreamers (most often female) as the recipients of help.

The rescue fantasy plays into ideational representations of archetypal thinking in which the dreamer is seeking divine intervention by some godlike presence, some unbeatable Superman or Zorro character. The dreamer is looking to be rescued by someone vaguely subversive (Rudolph Valentino in *The Sheik*) who doesn't necessarily have to play by societal rules and regulations, because the dreamer is usually feeling emotionally bereft and betrayed because of an adherence to the societal standards imposed and typified by the happy conjugal couple. The fantasy itself is that either intractable familial problems will be solved (by the aforementioned divine intervention) or that the unhappily married spouse will be pulled from the rootedness of a parched marriage thirsting for water. Similarly, a newly divorced spouse will wish to be extracted from her sense of being forsaken or undesirable.

To be magically able to transcend one's worst nightmare is indeed a greatly desired wish-fulfillment. The savior of these dreams is usually depicted as diametrically opposed to the negatively viewed spouse and on some level may represent an idealized verion of the present or ex-spouse. With characteristic attributes of adoration, loyalty, uxoriousness, sensuality, excitement, and good looks the savior or rescuer is a hard act to follow. The most important feature of these dreams is that being rescued, even unconsciously, has the effect of raising the dreamer's self-esteem, as the dreamer, even momentarily, feels watched over, protected, and sought out (desired).

There is also the element of rebirth and the underscored desire to start anew, as rescuers are usually associated with the one who births, which is why male rescue fantasies often have as their saviors representations of idealized maternal goddesses. Albeit, some males envision themselves rescued by a paternal image of the highest order—God the father. Since the rescuing male at the core of most female fantasies must be as far from the existent commonality of men, he is also typified as the supernormal male being who transcends all others.

The following male rescue fantasy dream was dreamt by a therapist, **A. N.,** just before his relationship breakup:

I was on some island . . . walking down the street (maybe it was Rio de Janiero) and there was a festival. There were long snakes (they were dead) that were attached to sticks that were held up in the air by people. Then, I find myself in a room. The room has open windows. The wind is hitting me in the face and I am rising from the bed. The room is on top of this mountain. Then, suddenly I'm on a beach and I see a huge clock. The sun

was like a clock, and I saw a man dressed all in black.
The man pointed to the sun. Then I saw the sun rising.

The island is the metaphorical land of the all-important male ego or I. The festival is in celebration of the self, and in particular the male self, as long snakes are being upheld (defended or affirmed in the face of a challenge)—the male phallus is raised to its ultimate length, its prominence is reinstated like a flag of male liberation.

Without any rhetorical philandering the phrasing "I find myself in a room" clearly states in regard to one's persona the intention of being found. The room (as mentioned) is the representation of the individual dreamer, and as such reveals the open windows of the eyes/soul in a posture of receiving. The wind is the elemental breath of life—the quickening force that elevates the dreamer rising from his bed or final resting place in a symbol of resurrection. The room, in an effort to surmount, sits atop the mountain, the summit, the pinnacle of strength, indestructibility, or immortality.

The dream visage changes from earth to water—from land to beach—and the surrounding water signifies mutability and new life. The sun as something that rises and sets is symbolized by a clock, which is presented as huge as time, endless and repeatable, caught in the roundness of its circularity.

The man in black is the animus, the Jungian male presence of wisdom in male consciousness—the spirit guide who perpetually points upward (the perpetual erection and excitation of becoming). The point of his pointing is also to administer invaluable instructions or lessons from above. The spirit of the dreamer is clearly rising away from any mundane earthly woes in the fortification of a mountainous masculine fulfillment.

With allusions to earth, wind, fire, and water, the dreamer

is rescued by his sense of wholeness in an elemental completion that is in harmony with the universe.

The following female rescue fantasy dream was dreamt by **Jacqueline** during a difficult loveless marriage that was nearing divorce:

> *I was riding inside a coach when suddenly the door opened . . . I was swept out of the coach by a dark-haired handsome man on a horse. He was wearing a loose flowing turban over his head (the turban was blowing in the wind). He whisked me onto his white horse. I ride off with him into the desert sands without knowing where I am headed.*

Riding inside a coach symbolizes the fetal passenger carried in the womb. The door opens onto a new existence, as rebirth is wished for. The rescuer is viewed as the one that births. Swept out of the coach is an allusion to making a clean sweep of an old past. The handsome man is the male animus in the female psyche called upon for strength and fortitude—for he will lead the female psyche out of bondage.

Riding off into uncharted regions demonstrates that faith has overcome doubt and trust has vanquished suspicion.

Yet another female rescue fantasy dream, from the divorcing **Michelle,** is as follows:

> *The building I am in starts crumbling, falling apart. First the ceiling caves in and I can see the sky through it. Then the floor starts shaking. I am running toward the door, which is difficult to open from inside. Then a man pushes it in from outside and rescues me from the building.*

The crumbling building is the internal, fragile sense of the divorcing self deconstructing or collapsing (see Falling Apart Dreams). But once the ceiling or roof caves in (the last straw on the camel's back) the sky's the limit, as the sky is seen or understood in the postdesolate dawn of the unconscious dreaming being as an assurance that light is to follow (for out of darkness comes light).

The floor is shaking in a groundswell of inner turmoil—no longer on solid ground, the bottom will no longer hold and the destruction is complete. The dreamer is dependent upon looking for structure—a mental construction to hold on to in the exterior world. As a recipient of help, the dreamer's door must be opened from the outside, as the door is pushed in from the outside (which is a sexual allusion). A new romantic attachment (the construction of an ideational male persona) is what is wished for and conceived of as being a panacea. The dreamer is rescued from the shattering and disintegrating structure of her marital relationship. To survive she must vacate (divorce) the premises. The dream states in no uncertain terms: "Michelle has left the building."

The following rescue fantasy dream was dreamt by author and astrologer **Robin MacNaughton** just before her divorce was to be finalized:

I have been living at the edge of woods for a very long time and am preparing to move. I am standing in the woods talking to a man who lives nearby. I don't know him very well. I am just aware that he lives nearby. He is Indian and a heart surgeon. As we talk, we see people walking through the woods at a distance. He calls my attention to them. They are walking in a procession, about to make a pilgrimage to a sacred temple in the heart of

*the woods. I say to the doctor, "I hear there is a sacred
temple in these woods. Is that true?" He laughs merrily
and says of course. I am fascinated. I ask him if he has
ever been there. Again he laughs and says of course, all
the time. He tells me that sometime he will take me to the
temple. I say, "All this time I have lived at the edge of
these woods, for so very long, but have never gone to the
temple. And now I am moving away." He smiles and
says, "That's okay. You'll still go."*

Robin's rescue fantasy dream evaluates her past and reexamines the amount of time spent living on the edge, which
symbolically refers to the edginess, the nervous anxiety of living in a bad marriage. Yet, from the very beginning, the tran-
scendent aspect of the dream is signified, as the dreamer is
prepared to move on. The woods (phonetically rendered as
would) represent the questioning and conditional nature of
this step toward freedom.

The heart surgeon is the rescuer, the one who mends broken hearts and symbolizes the spirit guide (the animus, the
male presence in the female psyche) who will walk the
dreamer through this pivotal point in her life in a pilgrimage
to a sacred temple. When the dreamer bemoans that she will
not be able to go to this sacred place because she is moving
away, the doctor reassures her that she will still go in, that the
sacred temple is within the dreamer. The Indian doctor who
brings back Robin's life is purposefully Indian, as being Indian presupposes the belief in reincarnation.

Yet, the dreamer is rescued by looking inside herself,
where she has never gone, into the woods of the unconscious.
Her attention is called to the sacred temple in the heart of the
woods—the sacred spiritual place, which is reparative, within
the heart.

21

Dreams of Physical Change: Becoming Someone New

In a geological analogy, a divorce, brought on by great heat or underlying pressure, causes an eruption, an alteration in psychical composition or structure that brings about a transformation of sorts; it changes markedly the appearance or form of one's original selfhood. This phenomenon often manifests itself in the unconscious in the format of dreams of physical change.

Whereas marriage produces a validation of existence, a verification of an individual's role in society, divorce engenders an endemic insecurity of selfhood—the divorcing couple lose their capacity to command emotional allegiance. Whereas marriage renders dependency by allowing the sense of selfhood to thrive on its emotional consumption of spousal love and approval, divorce hands in its resignation of the conjugal self. Thus, the flight from marital acceptance ruffles one's feathers to the extent that divorced spouses no longer feel physically or psychologically secure in their skins—they begin to examine themselves for signs of stress-related aging or anesthetized vitality.

In the severing of marital unions in which one has made inept efforts to repair a relationship, there is always an inherent feeling of failure that is oftentimes attached to a sense of guilt—the guilt and failure components conjoin a moral sense of inferiority that is concretized and thus made physical.

Divorce is a nihilistic state of disrepair that expels the bifurcated self back to its emotionally disadvantaged singularity, its truncated existence. The consequences are dire. The self is an amputee—one limb of vociferous and emotive consciousness is missing, having left in its place a phantom pain of underabundant love, self-esteem, and self-worth. (The physicality of the self is critiqued as insufficient.)

Divorced spouses not having met with spousal approval develop an insecurity regarding their desirability, self-esteem, and self-worth that necessitates some form of protective mediation on the part of the ego, which in certain instances the dream reveals to us in its wish for the nullification of the former married self. There is this exodus from the conjugal identity, as it failed the self the first time. Self-image is no longer valued or trusted, as this marital identity was not operational. In search of new air to breathe the old sense of physical presence flees as from a doomed planet. Sometimes the flight is to a surgeon's office for plastic surgery or reconstruction, as it were (see Actualized Dream of Jocelyne Wildenstein).

All things considered, the divorce event often initiates a metamorphosis in the unconscious dream in an attempt to repudiate the former spousal self-image—to repugn the self-effacement that comes from having failed in the marital arena.

Just after her divorce, the beautiful and very social brunette **Fern** had the following dream of physical change:

I went to the hairdresser and told her to remove the color from my hair. I told her to make me a platinum blonde like Marilyn Monroe. I also cut my hair short. Then I went to my exercise class unnoticed. No one recognized me.

Within the cutting of the hair (the truncated sense of self) a weakness is revealed, as this symbolizes the mythic Samsonian loss of power. Whereas going from dark to light represents the antithesis in physical appearance, it may also symbolize the desire to remove oneself from the darkness of despair to the lightness of happiness or being. Removing the color from the hair also suggests the wish to eliminate the fiery vivaciousness of Fern's persona—all traces of her former self.

The image of Marilyn Monroe is invoked and duplicated for purposes of desirability. The dreamer exercises to rid herself of a bad situation—a weight she carries around—but also to become less of who she was.

Not being recognized points to the dreamer's feeling of insignificance, of not being recognized for who she is or once was (while divorced, her role is unclear and ill-defined). Yet, on another level, to go unnoticed means that there is also the wish of forgetfulness and anonymity, as the dreamer does not want to be recognized even to herself as a divorced person.

During her divorce proceedings, **Maria** dreamt the following dream of becoming someone new:

> *I dreamt that I was in a battlefield. There were multitudes of soldiers everywhere. From a tent I was handing out papers or orders, as I was in command. I was wearing a military uniform . . . a long coat and trousers that seemed like the clothing that I had seen Napoleon wear in pictures. There were no women around and the way I was treated I think I was a man.*

Whereas the battlefield symbolizes the courts of the divorce, what is more important is that the dreamer seems to be holding court as she is handing out papers or orders, officiating in what appears to be a position of command. Thematically, the dreamer has a commanding presence (the wished-for ideal).

There is a military strategy to being in charge, as the dreamer wears the uniform of war. The masculine articles of clothing, the long coat and trousers, are associated with the qualities of leadership, great strength, and cunning, as they are historically linked to Napoleon.

The fact that there are no women around signifies that this is a man's world, wherein a man's strength is the required fare; this is why the dreamer imagines or envisions herself a man. In this way the dream belies the dreamer's wish for physical change (to become someone new)—the wish for gender transformation assumes a diminished view of women's importance in society and reveals the dreamer's own sense of helplessness and ultimate dependency on others.

Yet another dream of physical change was dreamt by **Sally** as she was contemplating divorcing her philandering spouse:

I was downstairs in the bathroom of a restaurant, putting on my makeup. There were a lot of crayons there and I noticed that I was painting my face all over with bright colors. Suddenly my mother walks in and tells me I look awful. The dream locale switches to outside where I am sitting on the lawn. When I get up to leave I notice the bottom of my dress is stained from the grass.

Downstairs in the bathroom is foremost a womb symbol and second a reference to a difficult and remote self-scrutiny, as the mirror is an implied symbol. The restaurant carries the womb image further in its attempt to get nourishment from the mother, the primary love object. The regressive element continues in its use of the crayons, which have the effect of covering over or distorting the dreamer's sense of physical presence, no doubt in an effort to avoid the unpleasantness of the moment (her contemplation of divorce). In effect, the dreamer is making up a new image or persona that the dreamer, who notices, is cognizant of. The wish for a brighter vista is clarified by the bright colors the dreamer paints herself with.

A validation of any desired physical change is needed, which is why the mother confers her disapproval. This serves to indicate the poor self-image of the dreamer (most probably heightened by her husband's philandering), for Sally is stained from her soon-to-be-broken marital relationship. Like a marked woman, the illusion holds that Sally is stained in a place where people can see. But importantly, the stain is externally caused and not self-attributed.

PART IV

**Divorce
Dreams of
Children of
Divorcing
Parents**

22

Burying the Head Dreams

According to Freud, dreams of young children are for the most part undisguised and transparent—their imagery and symbols easily interpretable. This is because children always dream of wish-fulfillments that pertain to their everyday subjective impressions and experiences that remain unsatisfied. Usually it is the case that whatever fears, longings, or anxieties the child is experiencing will manifest themselves in their dream states. The dream, therefore, hoping to find some solution (as a means of defense) to whatever in reality seems unobtainable, will also clearly depict the inner emotion of the dreamer.

In that these childhood dreams are short and to the point, coherent and easy to understand, they keep distortion at a minimum. Because there is not much resistance, the repressed wishes often surface into consciousness. More often than not, the symbolic significance is understood in terms of the dream imagery and its connection to the dreamer's immediate world, which is to say that the dream will reflect the events of the child's life.

As a dream is the mental reaction to prior experience (the day residue), the dream may be viewed as that which has left the child feeling some regret, a wishful element superseding any former longing. To this extent, any negative mental stimuli (such as the witnessing of volatile parental arguing) will disturb or disrupt sleep with the production of a dream reaction.

When a volatile marital relationship is the determinant of the childhood anxiety dream, the child, in reaction to its ego threat, will try to disavow what has been painfully acquired during consciousness. The ideational phrase "I do not want to see or hear my parents quarreling" is the wish that instigates a dream—the content of the dream is the satisfaction of that wish or need: "I will bury my head so I will neither see nor hear the quarrels of my parents." Thus, the passive wish is transformed into physical action (a dreamed experience) in order for the dream to remove or get rid of the problematic stimulus.

As divorce is known to have traumatic ramifications on one's sense of self within the structure of the family unit, it is easy to understand how an excess of negative stimuli would be perceived as threatening one's very existence. The defensive reaction of the child's ego to divorce is either to assume situational denial, add repression to its repertoire of protective ministrations, and/or to disavow by closing its eyes—which is why dreams of burying the head are frequently dreamt by children of divorcing parents.

The recurring burying-the-head dream dreamt by **Lara** during the breakup of her parents' marital relationship is as follows:

I saw a cartoonlike ostrich burying his head in the desert sand. He was all alone and standing on one leg. So familiar was this ostrich that from the moment I saw him I was certain that I had seen him before in a cartoon I had seen on television, but I was never able to prove this in reality.

Judged at a glance, the negative mental stimulus in Lara's home environment has been gotten rid of directly with the submergence of the head, for burying the head precisely symbolizes the withdrawing of interest from the world. Thus, the dream makes short work of the offensive stimulus—it shuts it out.

The cartoon ostrich substitutes for Lara as it provides her with the immortality and indestructibility of cartoon figures whose pliant forms can withstand any physical or mental contortions. As form follows function, the ostrich (with its neck-and head-burying skills) is the bird of choice.

The solo ostrich indicates that isolation is preferred over any gathering—getting away from it all is the ideal. As the bird's nature from time to time brings it to stand on only one of its legs, the ostrich fits into Lara's emotional schema, as it reveals that she sometimes feels as though she is standing on her last leg. (This realization never actually makes it into consciousness, which is why the ostrich is familiar but never actually proven to be seen by Lara.)

Another burying-the-head dream was dreamt by **Cornelia** after her parents' divorce:

> *I was in my grandmother's garden when I saw a groundhog digging up the dirt. It was making a hole behind the shrubbery. It crawled into the hole and I was worried that I would not see it again.*

The groundhog is yet another animal that burrows and submerges its presence, indicating once again the desire to withdraw from the world—to seek isolation. But the groundhog adds another dimension to this burying-the-head dream in that the notion of a shadow element is symbolically implied, if not present. In that the groundhog retreats only when it has not seen its shadow, Cornelia's sense of self-identity is diminished, which is why she is worried that she will not see it again (the groundhog is a symbolic substitute identity for Cornelia).

Making a hole has the phonetic rendering of *whole* and suggests that Cornelia wishes to become whole again, not only in regard to her autonomy, but also as a defense against the splitting action of her parents' divorce (her divided sense of self).

The grandmother's garden is symbolically a womb of a different color—a womb that makes a generational skip as it disinvolves Cornelia's mother from the scene (the womb of Cornelia's divorced mother is deemed unsafe because there is no father on the receiving end). Going back into the womb, however, reveals more than just the elemental wish to escape or the desire for protected nurturing in that a rebirth is also implied, which means that Cornelia will be born again as her mother in an attempt to regain identification with the maternal ideal.

23

Dreams of Being Killed Off: Identification with Parents' Pain

Dreams of being killed off are often reversals of the unconscious wish to kill—a wish that derives from a rising level of frustration that culminates in the need to aggress. (Within these dreams the aggression is projected outward.) These dreams have a purgatorial quality in that there is a cathartic release of pent-up anger and/or frustration directed at the perceived aggressor (the dreams point fingers and place blame on whomever is presented as being threatening to a child's environment).

Although these dreams appear to deliver punishments they are actually self-punishments wherein the dreamers become victims by their own hands (as a form of wish-fulfillment). Inwardly these dreams are dreamt in order that they be told—in order for guilt to be transferred and exteriorized. If a dream of being killed off could speak it would voice its recrimination, "Look what you have done to me."

As an approaching divorce can confer upon a woman the sense of morbidity or mortality, she may give off distress signals that are picked up or received by her children, who are desperately looking for cues in an increasingly unstable and unfathomable world. Often there is an identification with a parent's pain (a reciprocal identification).

The following dream of being killed off was dreamt by **Melissa** during the breakdown of her parents' relationship, just prior to the divorce, which she knew was eminent. The dream reveals Melissa's identification with her mother's pain:

> *I was standing with my father and brother alongside a lake with alligators in it. They were threatening to throw me in and feed me to the alligators. They did throw me in and they were laughing about it.*

Lines of demarcation are drawn (indicating a familial split), as Melissa dreams of herself standing with her father and brother. The lake is filled with predators—the alligators symbolize the fear of being swallowed up, which translates into the fear of loss of identity or selfhood. As Melissa is thrown into the dangerous waters of her unconscious there is the realization and fear of disembodiment and physical detachment. She has been thrown into the urgency of the divorce situation wherein she must sink or swim (eat or be eaten). Within Melissa's dream the threat that is made is also carried out.

The point in which Melissa falls victim to the men in her world is the moment of identification with her mother's pain and disintegration. As part of the divorce process, she will be chewed up and spit out in pieces by what appears to be a drastic alienation of male affection. Yet, Melissa accepts her physical death as something expected, in what appears to be her societal weltanschauung (a German concept roughly translated as worldview) wherein men rule. Thus, death brings the whole nasty situation to an end. Such is the threat of divorce!

24

Dreams of Being
Lost or Abandoned

During a divorce, dreams of being lost or abandoned are common motifs in the unconscious minds of children who feel as though they are losing their sense of security, their familiar place in the family. This notion of being lost is a palpable fear, as it hones in on the original birth trauma of separation anxiety wherein being lost is associated with death. Additionally, there is the frequent witnessing of fathers disappearing from the home, and the sense of an alienation or abandonment of affection between the parents. Just as a personal identity is being found it must be lost, as the total family picture has changed.

The divorce-induced fear of loss, or abandonment, schema has at its core the terrifying fear of no longer being loved. The expectation of familial nurturing is no longer perceived as being one that is tangible in that the divorcing, mutually rejecting spouses have already demonstrated a reciprocal withdrawal of affection. The child perceives this attitudinal and behavioral change as threatening, as it deviates from the ideal of unconditional love and acceptance.

Fears of loss of love, or abandonment, are also inextricably tied to evaluative concerns about self-worth or performance. In these divorce environments children often feel that they will not measure up to familial expectations, and a sense of vulnerability follows because they have lost their sense of control (they now fear that they will be disapproved of and dropped).

The following dream of being lost was dreamt by **Dorothy** during her parents' divorce proceedings:

I was in a large department store and I was holding the hand of my mother. There were many people all around and I was looking at toys and games and not particularly paying attention. Suddenly I looked at the person whose hand I was holding and it was a stranger. I could not figure out how I got in this situation. I was horrified. I looked around but my mother was nowhere to be found.

The intimate and personal familiar world of the family is transfigured (by the divorce) into a public and impersonal unfamiliar large department store, which is why holding the hand of the mother takes on such significance—it is the only remaining symbolic attachment to security. The hand is the symbolic umbilicus reunited with its fetal memory.

Getting lost in a world of toys is the dreamer's wish to disavow her situation by not paying attention. Yet being lost in the shuffle of the many people around is the dream warning of the dangers of not holding on to one's ideals. In a world of chaos it is easy to get lost or to lose oneself in all the wrong details. The dreamer reveals that she cannot figure out how she got into the situation of being lost—how the divorce came about. The dream signifies the horror of anonymity and depersonalization that the breakup of the family home ushers in. The unfamiliar hand of a stranger symbolizes that the divorce has made the dreamer seem a foreigner in her own land—desperately holding on to something that now seems estranged.

PART V

Actualized Dreams of Predivorced and Divorced Spouses

25

What is an Actualized Dream?

Unlike a dream that occurs in our unconscious minds during periods of deep sleep, an actualized dream occurs during consciousness—with our eyes wide open. It is defined as an extreme act—a deliberate behavioral acting out of a fantasy, during consciousness, wherein the unconscious aim is to fulfill an instinctual desire or wish. An actualized dream can be visualized as an escaped id that has just locked the door on the superego (our conscience) in an attempt to permit an unconscionable behavioral act to occur—an act that would surely be sublimated or suppressed (forbidden) in the world of consciousness. It is theorized that such a behavioral act, which I have termed an actualized dream, may be given psychoanalytic interpretation much in the same manner as dream analysis. (See actualized dream interpretations of Diana, Princess of Wales; Jocelyne Wildenstein.)

As sleep dreams have a moral purpose such as consolation, repudiation, rebuke, or self-affirmation, so must the wakeful actualized dream. But whereas a dream is a passive internal expression of unconscious fulfillments—making known what has been repressed in the unconscious—the actualized dream is active, unrepressed, externally expressed, and it takes place during consciousness. The action has motive and is a meaningful representation of failed repression. What is behind the wakeful action, the behavior, the image, ought in theory to be analyzed in the same manner as a dream—as the actualized dreamer is the dream itself and thus the symbolic content. The narrative has been discarded for the purely visual.

The cause of the extreme action may be found in the psycho-emotional disposition of "the actualizer" (herein Diana, Princess of Wales, etc.). This disposition is a result of the individual's psychic past; life events that trigger strong emotional responses leave heavy-handed imprints on thoughts and actions. For example, the divorce of the parents of Diana Spencer and/or the philandering of her husband, Prince Charles, were indelibly etched in her psyche.

The actualized dream is the opposite of a sleep dream that realizes or fulfills a wish in the unconscious world of fantasy—this is a fantasy realized or fulfilled in conscious reality. And unlike a dream, the actualized dream can be reproduced and remembered with accuracy. The reason behind the act may or may not be understood by the actualizer in that an action supersedes the thought behind it. Every action is motivated from the wish that something should or should not happen—as the action is the struggle for the realization of a wish. But one must first examine the purpose of an action, and what effect it is supposed to have. As the action is the aftereffect of the cause—the shock waves after an earthquake—the action should reveal the seismic shift beneath the fault line, the malaise beneath the symptom.

Like a sleep dream, the actualized dream rectifies a situation, but it does so not only by symbolic expression but by physical manifestation in the realm of visual consciousness. Therefore, nothing is expressed in disguised form, nothing is hidden—what you see is what you get. The following is an example of an actualized dream.

26

Actualized Dream of Diana, Princess of Wales

*Shortly after Christmas, January 1982, the three-months pregnant Diana throws herself down a wooden flight of stairs in front of her retreating husband, Prince Charles. (*Diana, Her True Story, *Andrew Morton)*

Here, the actualized dream of Princess Diana permits an unconscionable act—Princess Diana throws herself down the stairs in a symbolic attempt to descend the throne of England. The act is the opposite of ascending the throne or royal ascension in general. The loss of footing symbolizes that Diana has lost her emotional foothold in marriage. The actualized dream occurs on a flight of stairs which reveals the wish of flight, to flee from her distressful situation. The stairs are part of the symbolic representation, which allows them interpretative scrutiny. The stairs symbolize the wish for all to see, as *stairs* is a phonetic rendering of *stares*.

The actualized dream occurs during pregnancy because the pregnancy has become a physical symbol of a psychological state of anxiety—the Princess has been emotionally violated, tampered with. The pregnancy also symbolizes a pregnant pause, an uncomfortable silence, a hiatus in her love relationship. The wish of the actualized dream is to sever ties, to detach the placenta from the umbilical cord, to eliminate any royal connection. Diana, symbolically tied to the baby within, identifies herself with an innocence that Charles has already done away with. By deliberately throwing herself down the stairs and thereby risking miscarriage, Diana's actualized dream symbolizes the following message: "There is no room for the both of us; one must be killed off"—a reference to Camilla, mistress of the philandering Charles. Similarly, the miscarriage (which did not actually occur in reality) is nevertheless viewed as the underlying wish of the actualized dream action, as it symbolizes a miscarriage of justice. The miscarriage, in turn, would rob Prince Charles of his heir, which has the phonetic rendering of *air*—meaning his breath. Finally, Diana would take his breath away!

Throwing herself down the stairs metaphorically symbolizes Diana in the throws of emotional difficulty—thrown off track—as she is lacking in judgment. Throwing herself in the direction of the retreating Charles is the actualized dream's attempt at displacement, as Diana would like to displace her misery onto her husband. By replacing the word *throwing* with *hurling,* we are reminded of Diana's bulimia—her numerous throw-ups that symbolize the wish to rid herself of something distasteful that cannot be tolerated, to get something out of her system.

27

Actualized Dream of
Jocelyne Wildenstein

*During the breakup of her marriage Jocelyne Wilden-
stein has extensive facial surgery to make herself look
like a lion. (George Holz photo appeared in the 15 December 1997 issue of* New York Magazine.*)*

Jocelyne's behavioral act—altering her facial features to
achieve the inhuman image of a cat—is her actualized dream.
Choosing to look like an endangered species, specifically the
lion, is the dream symbol. The interpretation is as follows:
The wish to alter one's appearance to the point of loss of
recognition symbolizes the need for transformation and can
be seen as an attempt to nullify a present situation or state of
being (the divorce event).

Giving oneself the features of a wild beast is a desperate
attempt at gaining power over one's situational environment.
It must be noted that Jocelyne is the estranged wife of Alec
Wildenstein, son of the world's richest art scion, and owner of
Wildenstein Gallery in New York City. (Alec has left her for
another woman.) It also must be noted that Jocelyne had first
met her husband (formerly an avid hunter) during a lion hunt
at Ol Jogi, his family ranch in Kenya. It also bears mentioning that Alec is now a wild game conservationist. Bearing in
mind these facts allows us to interpret Jocelyne's actualized
dream as the wish for the preservation or conservation of her

marriage, as she is now the very beast her husband is seeking to protect.

But the transition from hunter to conservationist marks a symbolic change in her husband's attitude: ownership is no longer important—the chase has lost its seductive value. Similarly, what was formerly sought after (as Jocelyne once was) and set trap for is no longer violated but rather given its freedom. Therefore, Jocelyne's actualized dream seeks to stimulate once again Alec's waning passion to collect the wild, rare, and unobtainable—the exotic species that she has become. After all, in that she has violated herself through surgery she therefore opts for captivity.

In other words, the one thing the Wildensteins still have in common is their love of Africa and things wild—thus, Jocelyne becomes a wild thing. Her disfiguring surgery is viewed as a manifestation of her wild and impassioned nature in the hopes that once exposed this nature will inevitably prove attractive to Mr. Wildenstein.

Similarly, becoming a lion has the unmistakable value of giving Jocelyne the upper hand, as it imbues her with a powerful presence whose essence is not fully understood. Because Jocelyne has physically transcended the human realm and has entered the realm of the beast, she is no longer a fathomable entity and may thus be able to fascinate, to awe her bored husband. Her facial transfiguration reveals the extent of her alienation from humanity. The idea of divorce may have shattered Jocelyne's ego to the point where she may no longer be able to compete on a human level.

Yet, Jocelyne's extreme act may be considered one of self-preservation, for it is the lioness who does the killing, the lioness who has been termed a noble beast. She has after all lionized herself in her own eyes.

Lastly, the name *Wildenstein* has symbolic significance in

that the word *wild* is encased within it. The word *stein* means mug in German and face in British slang. By being a wild face, Mrs. Wildenstein retains her married name by physically embodying and personifying it, which is her hidden desire. This symbolically suggests that Jocelyne will always be a Wildenstein—even more so than Mr. Wildenstein!

PART VI

**Dream Motifs:
Five Typical
Love
Visitations
of the
Deceased**

Some say that gleams of a remoter world
Visit the soul in sleep,—that death is slumber,
And that its shapes the busy thoughts outnumber
Of those who wake and live.

PERCY BYSSHE SHELLEY

Such souls, whose sudden visitations daze the world,
Vanish like lightning, but they leave behind
A voice that in the distance far away
Wakens the slumbering ages.

SIR HENRY TAYLOR

How fading are the joys we dote upon!
Like apparitions seen and gone.
But those which soonest take their flight
Are the most exquisite and strong,—
Like angels' visits, short and bright;
Mortality's too weak to bear them long.

JOHN NORRIS

For in that sleep of death what dreams may come
When we have shuffled off this mortal coil
Must give us pause . . .

WILLIAM SHAKESPEARE

28

Consolation Love
Visitation Dreams

FILLING A VOID

Visitation dreams are a bridge to a continuing relationship not in the realm of the physical (actual/conscious) reality but in the realm of the unconscious psyche. These compensation dreams, which are engendered from personal need, occur in five different forms: (1) consolation love visitation dreams are dreams that may be conceptualized as valentines—emotional and sentimental emollients rubbed into the aching muscle of the heart (see Victoria Principal), (2) warning love visitation dreams are dreams wherein deceased loved ones enter the dreamer's dream state with the express purpose of warning the dreamer of a dangerous future situation that may be avoided (see M.), (3) instruction love visitation dreams are dreams wherein lessons are learned and dreamers are given guidance, counsel, and advise (see Brooke Astor), (4) inspiration love visitation dreams are dreams that are muselike, offering creative inspiration (see Mrs. L.), and (5) prophetic love visitation dreams are dreams that have prescience and foresight, often predicting impending deaths.

Whereas these forms are frequently known to occur within the realm of the psychological, where the wish is one of reparation or self-consolation, they are also thought by many (spiritualists and occultists included) to occur within a paranormal framework where the living, dreaming mind (or receiver) is viewed as a perfect vehicle for the deceased to enter or transmit, much in the same manner that a radio frequency is picked up from far away.

It has often been said that it is better to have loved and lost than never to have loved at all, but this in no way makes it any easier to deal with the loss of a loved one. This explains why there are so many consolation love visitation dreams. For even after long periods of mourning the loss of a loved one still leaves a void, a hollow feeling of emptiness that the mind often fills by piecing the loved one into its missing heart-shaped jigsaw space—for the dreamworld wants closure or completion. Dreams that offer another glimpse of the deceased make available the opportunity for communicative interaction via dream narration and visualization, which, in turn, evokes a transient moment of resolution that brings comfort and peace to the dreamers. Yet, the question remains—are these dream visitations actual reappearances of the dearly departed or have they been manufactured by needy dreamers as part of their elaborate coping strategies (protective measures) in a willful effort to fill the gaping hole of personal loneliness and loss?

Since there is no scientific validity or proof of the interaction of the dead with the living, perhaps the ineffable presence of soul after death can only manifest or present itself in dream experiences or visitations. To this extent what seems like paranormal dreams may have their roots in a subjective meaning as well.

For example, the following dream is either an authentic love visitation dream of consolation (in the sense of the paranormal) wherein the deceased Andy Gibb actually revisits his ex-lover Victoria Principal while she is sleeping, with the express purpose of comforting her with words that need to be said, or simply a dream that Victoria Principal gifts herself with in the hopes of soothing her raw emotions and thereby ridding herself once and for all of any residual guilt. You the reader must decide!

VICTORIA PRINCIPAL'S (CONSOLATION) LOVE VISITATION DREAM

In that we had never again spoken after the breakup, during my dream Andy came to me because he knew that I was haunted by this and we sat down and had the talk that I wanted to have, and we needed to have, and I thought it was so much like Andy to come back and do this. (VH1)

When a loved one suddenly dies there is always remorse over words that were left unsaid, conversations that were never had. And because the mind and heart demand closure, the dream process inevitably delivers—serving up a visitation wherein the deceased is brought back with the explicit purpose of settling unfinished business. In other words, this love visitation dream is a wish-fulfillment wherein the dreamer gifts herself with the presence of her loved one in a defensive attempt to end a melancholia that has persisted.

Victoria endows Andy with a thoughtful selflessness that at the time he was incapable of revealing due to his addiction to drugs (for given Victoria's real-life ultimatum: "It's either me or drugs," Andy would choose the latter). Victoria, by rewriting the event, makes Andy comply with her need to talk (which, in reality, he neither had the time nor inclination to pursue). The dream phrase "we sat down and had the talk" represents Victoria's strong need for communication, as sitting down to talk usually symbolizes a pivotal time in a memorable relationship between two people. (Note: seated at a round table indicates an intimate and agreeable relationship whereas seated at a square table suggests a relationship fraught with difficulty.) Victoria projects onto Andy her own want and need to be comforted, as she includes his need (by the use of the plural pronoun) in her own individual need to talk.

Metaphysically speaking, however, there is the distinct possibility that the deceased may find the unconscious mind a viable and accessible vehicle of entrance. As was previously stated, the sleeping mind, on those occasions when the unconscious mind has stripped away all the distractions and stimuli that the conscious mind is subject to, may act as both transmitter and receiver, much like a radio that is able to pick up unknown distant frequencies.

A FORM OF WISH-FULFILLMENT

It cannot be overstated that love visitations are the most sought-after dreams because they reunite the dreamer with a deceased loved one, particularly in cases of sudden deaths wherein the dream visitation alters time and makes possible the expression of feelings that have not yet found their outlet (not yet been revealed) and words that have not yet been uttered. The purpose of the visitation dream is to pave the way for emotional closure. But the visitation dream has another important function: it allows an ongoing communication with the deceased that eliminates any sense of futility and finality. The visitation dream establishes a bond or link with the deceased that makes one's mortality a less insufferable thought.

Dreaming of a deceased person reflects the wish for continuance, as it confers upon the dreamer a sense of immortality, for in the majority of narratives these dreams proclaim that no one dies, they just disappear from view. The visitation dream suggests that the world of consciousness is at odds with the internal psyche (soul) or essence of the personality that is invisible when apart from its fleshy exterior, the material body. The dream confirms that this immaterial spirit essence is still a reachable viable consciousness in the workings of the unconscious mind. Thus, the dream consoles our wakeful consciousness while stroking our emotional skins as it forms a reassuring solidified image of the hereafter and its constituents.

The dream concretizes an idea through its visualization of an image that the unconscious mind already knows or has foreknowledge of on some level of awareness—an idea that the conscious mind is not yet aware of. The dream seeks to inform by presenting unconscious insights into consciousness. But consciousness is what gets in the way of recognition. Therefore, we must never underestimate the intellect of the unconscious—the power of its skills. Nor must we dismiss the dream that broadens the boundaries of an unknown framework in the wish to integrate not just consciousness with unconsciousness but mortality with immortality. The following is an example of a consolation dream dreamt by a woman, **L.**, which contains gratifying conceptions of life in the hereafter:

My driver (who was deceased for one year) was walking toward me down the street, conversing with an older man. He smiled and said hello. He looked wonderful. He handed me my handbag. I had lost my bag and he had found it for me.

There is conversation and communication after death, as symbolized by the two men conversing. The banality of the situation is generated by the casualness of the conversation.

There is movement and activity as opposed to stasis in that the two men are walking—there is upright mobility. There is communion with others and therefore camaraderie. Sheer happiness is conveyed by a smile, hardiness by the driver who looks wonderful. Stability is established, as the two men are on the street with their feet on solid ground.

An aura of omnipotent wisdom is achieved, as the driver has found that which was not visually available—the missing handbag. The driver has given the emptiness of space a material and solid dimension. By giving back the handbag, the driver represents beneficence and a well-meaning orientation—he gives back that which is irreplaceable. The symbolic intention of returning a lost handbag is that it reissues the identity of the recipient, as a handbag symbolizes the sense of self, the individual persona. Thus, the dead are not to be mourned, as they are not the ones who are lost—we are. But, perhaps we *can* be found in our dreams!

SYNOPSIS OF CONSOLATION AND REASSURANCE

In reality: driver is both loser and object lost.

In the dream: driver is both finder and object found. He finds the dreamer (in the symbolic form of her handbag); he is found in that the dreamer encounters him.

Translation: **The dead are not lost but found. They give back what is taken away.**

Another example of a consolation love visitation dream was recently dreamt by **Soheir Khashoggi,** aunt of Dodi Fayed, several months after his tragic death:

CONSOLATION LOVE VISITATION DREAMS

Dodi and I are outside walking in the street. He is holding my hand. It is dusk. He is telling me that he is fine, and very much in love with Diana.

In order to interpret a dream it is most important to notice the way in which the dream is worded—the narrative structure—the way it is told. For example: the dream phrase "Dodi and I are outside" is very different from "I was with Dodi outside." Although the meanings of both phrases are inherently the same, the dream version (within the narrative text of the dream) expresses a definite connection. "Dodi and I" expresses the wish for symbolic correlation. In addition, in the dream version the threatening noun *outside* is kept away from Dodi's name; it follows after the word *are,* as outside represents the detachment of the world of the deceased, which is outside of the realm of the living. The nondream version connects Dodi with outside.

The wish for connection is continued, as Dodi is holding Soheir's hand. The holding of hands symbolically establishes a link like a daisy chain—they are together, now and forever. Even though this is a consoling love dream visitation, the symbol of dusk reveals Soheir's continual mourning. The consolation comes from Dodi expressing his well-being and his love for Diana, Princess of Wales. Once again, the dream is either a wish-fulfillment of the grieving Soheir to commune with her beloved nephew, or a genuine visitation from the world of the deceased. The answer, unfortunately, cannot be confirmed within the pages of this book.

The following consolation love visitation dream was dreamt by **Geoffrey Bloomingdale,** son of Betsy and Alfred Bloomingdale, many years after his father's death:

I dreamt that my deceased father was at the car races on the track, racing his stock car. He had entered three races but I don't think he won.

In a typical example of a consolation love visitation dream, Geoffrey envisions his father racing because he would like to feel that his father still has drive and its associate implication, ambition. His father is visualized as being revved up and ready to go; he is still living life in the fast lane wherever he is. Being on the track is the wish that Geoffrey can track or locate his deceased father's whereabouts but also signifies that his father continues on track as opposed to being off track or out of the loop. It makes no difference that Geoffrey's father does not win the race; what matters is that he is still in the running and that progress is being made. The dream concerns itself with the kind of movement associated with things living as opposed to the stasis associated with things inanimate or dead.

As a true consolation visitation, the dream carries the message that failure (as symbolized by death) should not be viewed as a deterrent—one should try, try again. An instructional element in the dream places a value on competing in life's challenges in that the father (in visitation form) seeks to inspire and spur on his son.

Dreams of visitations from the deceased are the most satisfying and usually the most profound dreams, as messages are usually passed along—advice, reassurance, or consolation is given. Often the dreamers awaken with a sense of awe, or just a general feeling of happiness. These dreams are wishes to send and to receive communication from beyond the mundane world of the living. They reestablish faith in the hereafter, as they offer the assurance of continuance. Most important, they present the idea that no one ever dies.

The following consolation love visitation dream was dreamt by **Elvis Presley,** whose twin, Jesse, was stillborn at birth, as told to Larry Geller—personal hairstylist, spiritual mentor, and close friend of Elvis's—at Graceland:

I had this dream that The Presley Brothers were performing. My twin brother, Jesse, and I were onstage, both wearing white jumpsuits, with guitars slung around our shoulders. He was the spitting image of me except he could sing better.

As losing a twin can produce what is called *survivor's guilt* in the twin that remains, it is not surprising that Elvis Presley would dream of sharing the incredible phenomenon of his fame and even his talent with his stillborn brother Jesse. What is interesting, however, is that Elvis endows his brother with a better singing voice, and this is what brings spiritual meaning to the dream, the implication being that the brother's voice is coming from another place—of heavenly timber, tone, and resonance.

Teaming up with one who has passed to the other side reveals the wish to be elevated to a higher level of existence, which is symbolized by the stage. The guitars around the shoulders may represent symbolic wings or angelic equipment, as this is an angelic scene from above—with singing voices, stringed instruments, and the color white representing spiritual wisdom and purity. Taken literally, the image of jumpsuits suggests that these are suits that jump or rise. Thus, the dream underscores Elvis's spiritual quest, as it reveals his wish to become one with a heavenly being or presence, to join with his twin other side, to become whole and thereby enlightened.

☾

The following consolation visitation dream was dreamt by
the very beautiful supermodel **Carmen:**

*It is winter. I am sitting on a park bench in the park with
my father (who is deceased). There is a blanket around
us, so we are not cold. My father tells me, "You will be
all right."*

As a concert violinist, Carmen's father would frequently
leave home to perform, leaving Carmen to await their many
wonderful walks in Central Park upon his return. By filling the
park with the warmth of her father's presence, and the warmth
of childhood memories, Carmen's dream reverses the chill and
bareness of winter—the season of leaving—for the wish of the
dream is to reunite with her deceased father and gain consolation from this reunion.

Even in winter there is warmth between father and daughter, a blanket is around them. The blanket represents security
and comfort and reflects the wish to be taken care of—tucked
in, covered, and protected. As the blanket is another symbol
for the father, Carmen is blanketed in love.

Sitting means it is not yet time to go; to park means to stay
in one spot. Poignantly, being benched means not allowed to
play—Carmen's way of making sure her father will not leave
her as he did in the past to play the violin. The park bench
symbolizes solidity and permanence, offering the consoling
reassurance of her father's words, "You will be all right," as
if to say, I am here with you always.

Daniel Straus, the CEO of Multicare, had the following
consolation visitation dream:

*My father appeared to me after his death, before I
started Multicare. I couldn't reach him. He was saying
something to me but I couldn't hear him. He called my
name. It was in an underground parking garage.*

Something underground, below or beneath the surface,
usually represents the unconscious, because it cannot be seen
from above. Thus, Straus's unconscious is trying to come to
terms with his father's death, his father's absence or invisibility. The underground parking garage symbolizes a graveyard
where his father is not buried but rather garaged as a parked
car; in that cars are only parked temporarily, his father may
again resurface or resurrect. The car also represents the future
vehicle of the journey to the other side, which animates and
vivifies that which has come to a halt.

Daniel's determination to reach the unobtainable shows
tenacity and willfulness. In a wish to communicate with his
father for consolation Straus has his father call out his name.
The name-calling is significant—an important symbol of
recognition that makes whole again the dreamer's newly fragmented sense of identity, as pieces of self often chip away
with the death of a loved one. Necessarily, Straus neither
hears nor understands what his father has said before because
only the name *Daniel* is meaningful in that it has the restora-
tive power of self-validation.

A most amazing and poignant consolation visitation dream
was dreamt by a friend of mine, **Antonia di Portago:**

*I am in the Parisian house I was raised in. I am told by
my mother's friend my mother will call me on the telephone. This shocks me, since I am aware my mother
died long ago. I stay next to the telephone, awaiting my*

*mother's call. I ask my late mother's friend for my
mother's telephone number, so I may call her myself.
The friend's response hurts me. She says my mother
doesn't want me to know where she is, even though she
is still alive. I ask her friend to tell me where she is, or
to take me to her, but to no avail. I try to call her any-
way. When we speak, she tells me she is not dead after
all, but is in hiding because she doesn't want any part
in life anymore, and she doesn't want anyone to know
she is alive, or where she is. She just wants to be left
alone. I ask to see her; I can't wait to run to her and fall
in her arms, but she refuses . . . even after I beg her,
crying, to let me see her.*

The dreamer wishes to speak to her deceased mother, and
by reversal, dreams her mother wants to call her. The telephone as a symbol of communication—of wanting to be connected with someone—conveys a voice from far away over
invisible wires. The telephone, which bridges the unseen/in-
accessible with the accessible, gives rise to associations with
those that have passed to the other side.

Mother's call can mean mother's telephone call, or, figuratively, an audible beckoning to return home, which may reflect the dreamer's depressive notion to reunite with her
deceased mother through dying. As is the case when a parent
dies, children often feel responsible—that they have done
something wrong to deserve abandonment. This engenders
feelings of guilt. Thus, Antonia punishes herself by dreaming
that her mother wants no part of her, as she does not want her
daughter knowing her whereabouts.

Being told her mother is alive is a wish-fulfillment. Wishing to be taken to her mother is again the depressive desire to
join with the mother. When the mother, who previously did

not want anyone to know she is alive, finally does the right thing and speaks to the dreamer, the mother makes it known that she is making an exception with Antonia. This has the effect of consoling Antonia's hard feelings, as she is made to feel special.

Although the dream denies the dreamer from running to her mother, and falling in her arms, which affirms the life instinct within the dreamer, thoughts of abandonment and rejection are indulged, in that the dreamer deliberately dreams of a mother unwilling to reunite with her child. This indulgence in rejection allows the dreamer to feel self-pity, which plays an important role in exonerating her guilt. The mother is the bad one, the one who hurts the feelings of the child. Thus, the dream ends positively with the dreamer's self-reconciliation and the expression of anger toward her mother for having died. In other words, the dream rids the dreamer of a guilt she may have been carrying all these years.

The following consolation and desire love visitation dream was dreamt by **Sir Winston Churchill** while he was attempting to paint a portrait of his father. The father suddenly appeared, seated in Winston's big red leather armchair in the artist's studio. However, in conferring with his grandson, Winston Churchill, I was informed that this dream of Sir Winston's was generally thought to be a reverie that occurred when Sir Winston was in a trancelike state. I was also informed that no record exists of Sir Winston ever having painted a portrait of his late father. This fact is insignificant, though, in that Sir Winston has revealed that the moment his father vanished he was too tired from the vividness of the illusion to continue painting. Therefore, the painting may never have been completed. Sir Winston was urged by his children, Randolph and Sarah, to write down the dream, which, in its written form seems an elaboration of the original dream or fantasy. Randolph Churchill has said *The Dream* was most uncharacteristic of his father's writings. Herein follows the gist of the dream—mostly paraphrased and greatly truncated:

> *I was painting in my studio. I had been sent a badly torn canvas portrait of my father, [Lord Randolph]. I thought I would try to make a copy of it. My easel was under a strong daylight lamp. On the right of it stood the portrait I was copying—behind me a large looking-glass, so that (I) could frequently study the painting in reverse. I must have painted for an hour and a half, and was deeply concentrated on my subject. I was drawing my father's face, gazing at the portrait, and turning round to check progress in the mirror. My mind was freed from all other thoughts except the impressions of that loved and honoured face on the canvas, on the picture, and in the mirror. I was just trying to give the twirl to his moustache when I turned round and there, sitting in my . . . upright armchair, was my father . . . just as I had seen him in his prime. . . . 'Papa!' I said. My father asked me to fill him in on what had transpired over the years. [A long conversation ensues where Lord Randolph hears his son recite the history of the twentieth century while ironically leaving out the one thing that would have amazed his father the most—that Winston had become Prime Minister during the most crucial period of his nation's history—that he rescued Britain and perhaps western civilization as well. What is strange, then, is that Randolph has stated that this dream or fantasy of his father's was probably inspired by Winston's regretting that his father would never know what he had achieved. But if this is so, why did not Winston mention*

all that he wanted? The father ends the conversation, saying among other things—that he never expected that Winston would have developed "so far and so fully"— that Winston should have gone into politics where he might "even have made a name for himself." The father gives Winston "a benignant smile," strikes a match to light his cigarette, and in that tiny flash, vanishes. Made tired by the illusion Winston notes that he cannot continue his painting—his "cigar had gone out, and the ash had fallen among all the paints."] (From The Dream *by Winston S. Churchill.* The International Churchill Societies, second edition, 1994)

The torn canvas portrait of Winston's father symbolizes that the fabric of memory is coming undone; therefore, Winston tries to improve his memory, to make a copy of it in order to keep his father's image alive in his mind's eye. Drawing his father's face represents the wish to pull forth the paternal persona. Studying the painting in reverse suggests that Winston wishes that his father were alive, that things would be seen as they are today. (Winston, having only been twenty years old when his father died had not yet come into his own, as he had done badly in school. His father often wondered what would become of him.) The mirror behind Winston symbolizes a reversal of image and represents his desire to examine the past.

Winston's father returns (in retrospect) in his prime at thirty-seven years old; Winston is a seventy-year-old man. In answering all of his father's questions, it is now Winston who is the instructor, the teacher, the knowledgeable one, which is perhaps why he modestly withholds the revelation of his personal success. The motivation behind Winston's most curious ellipsis seems to be that Winston did not feel himself worthy of competing with his father—for indeed his great achievements far exceed those of his father. It also seems certain that Winston does not want to intimidate his father but wants rather to remain somewhat mediocre in his father's eyes so as to retain or recapture the closeness that he felt during his early years. Another measure of consolation is that the dream is without hubris.

When Lord Randolph vanishes, Winston is too tired to continue painting, for the painting of the father is the physical erection of the male illusion. Winston cannot sustain the illusion—his cigar had gone out (the phallus, the male energy, depleted). The culmination is the ash, the end of the fire that is life. Perhaps this is the humble realization that Winston cannot, even in fantasy, praise his own accomplishments.

The ash is the reality of death, which has momentarily mixed with the tools of creation as represented by the paints. The ash is dry, the paints are wet. The ash is the father's ashes, which have fallen among the paints—the reality of the father's death momentarily blots out Winston's creative spirit.

The following consolation visitation dream is one that may be termed an indirect visitation wherein the dreamer views from afar the reemergence of his deceased father stepping out from the grave.

In 1849, several months after the tragic event of his father's funeral, **Friedrich Nietzsche** had the following dream. He was five and a half years old:

> *I heard organ tones as at a funeral. As I saw what the cause seemed to be, a grave opened up suddenly and my father climbed out of it in his burial clothes. He hurried into the church and came shortly out again with a child under his arm. The grave opened, he climbed in,*

*and the cover (sank) back onto the opening. At the same
time the organ tones fell silent and I (awoke). (From
Carl Pletsche's* Young Nietsche)

In this frightening nightmare (which has elements of a
negative consolation love visitation dream), the wish is
clear—Nietzsche wants to join his father in death. The father
is viewed as omnipotent in that he is seen to willfully come
and go from his own grave. This is meant to console and reassure the dreamer that death can be opened up or penetrated,
that it is not a fixed state of existence but rather a habitat of
choice. The grave opening symbolizes that the entrance to the
world of the deceased can be broken into.

The father hurrying out from the church with a child under
his arm, as though he has stolen it, symbolizes the loss of Nietzsche's childhood, as Nietzsche himself is the child. Indeed,
the father is metaphorically viewed as robbing Nietzsche of
his childhood joys.

Yet, on the day following Friedrich's visitation dream, his
younger brother, Joseph, actually dies and is buried in the
same coffin with his father—placed in his father's arms. What
are we to think as we now reexamine young Nietzsche's
dream. We can conclude that the dream was prophetic without altering the idea that Nietzsche's secret wish was to remain with and be protected by his father, for within the dream
the child that is carried out by the father is figuratively carried
off under his father's wing.

Yet, Nietzsche's consolation visitation dream may also be
viewed as a fulfilled wish of Nietzsche's to remove his only
male competitor from the Nietzsche household, for Joseph's
death makes Nietzsche the only male in the household. What
is more probable, however, is that Nietzsche suffered from
negative feelings of abandonment and lovelessness that made

him dream of his brother (and not himself) being whisked off by his imposing father as the object of his father's affection and devotion.

At the end of Nietzsche's dream the organ tones fall silent, which symbolizes that the music has stopped in young Nietzsche's life. When he says, "I awoke," it seems a telling realization: as if to say that he has awakened to the miseries of life, the sudden departures that leave one with feelings of loneliness and longing. Early on in the dream, when Nietzsche analytically says, "I saw what the cause seemed to be," he seems to be speaking about his own suffering and the negativity surrounding love, human weakness, and dependency—the hardship of mourning attached to the love of the departed.

The following consolation love visitation dream was dreamt by **Mrs. L.** a week after the unexpected loss of her close friend:

> *I was walking outside in the street with my friend L. Suddenly, while walking, he held me close and we started passionately kissing. It was so sudden that I still had some food in my mouth that I had been chewing. He said, "You know, you should have told me," and I said, "I couldn't, because it happened so soon and was so unexpected."*

Walking outside contains a subtle reference to the dead as it establishes the wish to cross boundaries—the boundaries between life and death. But another boundary is crossed: the move is made from platonic friendship to physical love. As friendship in the platonic sense represents the highest form of love in that it transcends its need for physical gratification (love of the material), it favors more spiritual or immaterial ends.

It should be noted that friendship sets up mutually respected interpersonal rules that infrequently transform its nature into something other than what it is. Yet, when a friend dies and is no longer physically accessible sometimes a new way of relating to him is desired.

The passionate kissing the dreamer engages in is shocking in that her desire was so unexpected (repressed). There is the implication, however, that for whatever reasons, sexual feelings had been deeply submerged as they never revealed themselves in consciousness. In this way the dream most emphatically reveals the dreamer's (and maybe even the deceased's) regret over words not spoken and feelings not shared.

Both the death of the deceased friend and the dreamer's romantic feelings are perceived as unexpected, as both happen too soon. The deceased, who disapprovingly says, "You know, you should have told me," not only refers to the fact that the dreamer had unswallowed food in her mouth but also serves as a reprimand—the deceased friend would have wanted to know that he was cared for romantically. This is the emotional revelation that the dreamer is unable to swallow. The dream, however, is a consolation visitation in that it gives the dreamer the chance to reveal to her deceased friend what perhaps she never would have told him even if there had been enough time.

From a paranormal perspective the deceased has returned to reveal his true feelings (romantic inclinations) to the dreamer—as a consolation—and to give the dreamer a last chance to respond.

The following consolation visitation dream was dreamt by **J.:**

My deceased mother and I were in a store alone. It was
empty. Suddenly a black man started insulting us, curs-
ing. I started to leave but my mother turned around,
lifted her skirt and showed her behind to him. I was em-
barrassed. She was wearing black nylon or rayon
drawers. They were a little bunchy. Like maybe she had
something in them. He came closer as if to sniff, star-
ing. "What did you do that for?" I asked when we left.
She replied, hurriedly, urgently, "I was doing what my
mother did to me."

Consolation seems to be derived from exposure, as the
dream both symbolically and literally seems to be airing its dirty
laundry in giving explanation as to why a dirty deed was done.

In conscientious manner, the deceased mother does her
duty—in more ways than one. Lifting her skirt to reveal that
she has soiled her drawers, she states, "I was doing what my
mother did to me." Even though the presumed bunchy excrement in the drawers establishes the mother's loss of control, it
also allows her to replace an absent father with a protective
stench.

By showing her behind the mother reveals a dark and ex-
cremental past. The implied message that appears to console
is that we often pass along generational hurts whether we
want to or not.

The black man is the integrated personality of the dreamer
who within the dream urgently tries to indemnify a narcissistic mother involved with her creation (the feces) by viewing
her act as the mirroring of a dutiful daughter.

The following consolation visitation dream was dreamt by
Heather Moore, disc jockey at WLVU in Florida, at a time in
her life when she was in need of being nurtured:

I dreamt that I was sitting in my deceased grand-mother's lap in the rocking chair of my youth as I used to do in the past except that now I am my present age. While I was telling her some problem and she was giving me advice she was braiding my hair.

The consolation behind the dream is to be small again and taken care of—to be responsibility-free. The gentle rocking back and forth of the chair, while being comforting, also symbolizes the movement from past to present and then back to past again and conveys the circularity of time. The back and forth movement signifies that life is not static but rather in a constant state of flux—and that what is perceived now as being a difficult period in one's life will change into a state of happiness. The braiding of the dreamer's hair represents to what extent she has entwined or incorporated her deceased grandmother into her life, and similarly, how she has preserved cherished memories of her youth.

The following consolation love visitation dream was dreamt by the former First Lady of Indonesia on the eve of her mother's death. As the mother was in a coma, she had not seen her daughter for the last nine months of her life. **Dewi Sukarno's** visitation dream recurred for forty consecutive nights. Her dream is as follows:

I am inside my house standing and speaking with my mother. I am complaining to her, "You are so naughty. You are hiding yourself from me. You have made me so sad but you are not really dead, you are alive." I hug her in happiness. But on the fortieth night when I hug her she was so soft and so light like a gem. Her body collapsed like a balloon without any air. There was no-body—nothing in my arms—and I screamed from fear.

Dewi's forty-day visitation dream conforms to the Buddhist and Christian beliefs that a departed soul will be earthbound for forty days. This defies any psychoanalytic interpretation, as this must be viewed as a spiritual and mystical experience that is beyond any form of scientific reasoning.

From an emotional, psychoanalytic perspective, however, Dewi's complaining and chastising ("You have made me so sad") reveal the anger one feels over the death of a loved one, as the death is seen as an abandonment and even as a betrayal. The protective device of denial kicks in that the dreamer would rather think of her mother as naughtily or mischievously hiding than come to grips with the reality of a deathly and permanent absence. The hugging is the desire to make the immaterial solid again—to regain physical contact by concretizing the abstract, which is a nullification of spirit. For thirty-nine days the dreamer is consoled by the presence of her deceased mother so that she happily goes to sleep each night in anticipation of a maternal visitation.

On the fortieth day, reality and acceptance sink in—the bubble bursts. There is the sad realization that there will be no more visitations, which is why the mother's body collapses like a balloon that has lost all its air (the breath of life). The illusion, soft and light, is entirely perishable. "There was nobody" means quite literally, there was no body—no earthly sign or manifestation of substance or form. Similarly, the dreamer screams because to have "nothing in my arms" signifies that there is nothing left to hold on to, which is a frightening thought.

From a paranormal perspective the deceased mother has left the mundane world in a serenity of enlightenment and with her daughter's blessing. As a form of relenting the dreamer's former anger is transformed into a spiritual acceptance of a higher truth. The dreamer has let her mother go on into the light.

The following recurring consolation visitation dream was dreamt by the former model and fashion editor of the French edition of *Harper's Bazaar,* **Pia Kazan:**

Years ago before my father died he sat in the garden of our house in the south of France apologizing that of all my fourteen siblings he had given me the least of all because he had thought me the strongest. This house is now mine and I have been wanting to sell it for a long while because it needs work and a lot of things. I have the recurring dream that my father is always fixing the house with me. He is back in the garden in St. Tropez where he is planting. He says, "Look, I planted you a garden and you will have beautiful flowers."

As the house represents the self, Pia incorporates her deceased father into her present life as a means of consolation. The garden is symbolic of what the father's love can grow (the continuance of love between father and daughter). The message is that the father has sowed the seeds of happiness. But if Pia is to flower she will have to look or pay attention to what life has given her. The father is fixing the house with his daughter in an attempt to fix or make amends for lost time, for not having given her much in the past.

On a paranormal level, the father returns in the hopes of dissuading his daughter from selling the house.

The following love consolation visitation dream was dreamt by **Ghislaine Absy** just after her uncle died when she was a young girl living in Beirut:

I had a dresser with a little chair next to my bed. I was facing the wall. My uncle was sitting in the chair. He was dressed in a suit and tie with his cane and he was staring at me.

In this consolation visitation the chair is what establishes permanence, as the chair is a solid structure. The uncle's cane symbolizes support. The staring function of the uncle establishes his watchfulness, as the dreamer wishes to be watched over, looked after, and protected. The dead are clothed in familiar wardrobe to establish the sense of continuance.

SELF-VISITATION: ANOTHER TYPE OF CONSOLATION DREAM

The whole phenomenon of near-death experiences that trigger out-of-body reactiveness—awareness or consciousness of the self from the viewpoint of the self—may be explained in terms of what I would like to call self-visitation dreams, wherein the dreamer (who is just a quark away from being deceased) has passed into another form of external unconsciousness that allows the dream to be experienced as real. In other words, the soul leaves the body for this brief moment in which the body is not habitable. (The accident produces simultaneously both the unconsciousness *and* the trauma that jolts the dreamer awake into a nonseeing, nontemporal, nonspatial perception or form of consciousness.)

Oftentimes unconscious victims of accidents have the experience of looking down at themselves (from an elevated point of view or perspective where they are hovering on the ceiling) lying on either a stretcher, operating room table, or sick bed while doctors or paramedics prod them with probes, take blood, administer IVs, and in general attempt to save them—to bring them back to the world of the conscious living. Many have the realization that it is not opportune to be outside of their bodies; these have assiduously (unconsciously) willed themselves back inside of whatever level of consciousness is available to them. This willful action is taken in the preservation of the self as we know it. Thus, that the deepest loss of consciousness through physical trauma may bring perceptions of outside external happenings as compensation may not be so incomprehensible.

Similarly, in a comatose state, in deep unconsciousness, the consciousness of the soul may leave the body in an attempt to impartially view what is happening during this trauma-induced consciousness, as a protective device. The consciousness I speak of, the consciousness of being outside oneself, has the objectivity to view the normally subjective unconscious of the being. It is theorized herein that some form of protective mediation may occur, as the body in coma cannot immediately define or defend itself.

Even Carl Jung has written that in cases of profound "injuries to the brain [or] in some states of collapse loss of consciousness may be accompanied by perceptions of the outside world and vivid dreams experienced." This may be perceived as the persistence of consciousness even in states of apparent unconsciousness.

What is the reality behind an out-of-body experience? The following self-visitation consolation dream was dreamt by **Laura Hunt** after a horseback riding accident in Texas left her unconscious and near death. A dust storm (a minitornado) had spooked her horse and sent him heading toward a five-foot fence. As the horse neared the fence he veered sharply to the left and Laura, prepared to jump, was flung at high speed into the fence. Laura's self-visitation dream follows:

*I am sitting up in the corner of the ceiling of a van (on
the way to the hospital), and looking down as I watch
this 250-pound woman paramedic put an IV into my left
arm. I hear her saying, "thirty over zero" and "We're
losing her." I said to myself, "Laura get in there, Hunt
get in there." Then I am in my chest. I couldn't move or
see anything as everything was dark, but my mind was
thinking.*

Twelve years later the dreamer still feels that she traded
life for a life lesson. That she could have allowed herself to
die then and there but that she opted to live again, with a new
enlightened perspective and in a different phase of spiritual
development.

As an actualized dream (see Actualized Dreams), the hitting of a wall was symbolic of coming to the end of the
road—to a dead end—as this was a pivotal point in the
dreamer's life. As the dreamer felt that she had the golden
touch, this event brought her in touch with her own vulnerability and mortality. Although the situation was out of the
dreamer's control, preparing to jump over the five foot wall
was like Icarus trying to fly to the sun, and perhaps like Icarus
her wings needed to be singed.

29

Warning Love Visitation Dreams

nother type of love visitation dream often contains a warning and is thus thought of as being protective in nature. But whether the dreamer is unconsciously aware of a danger that is repressed in conscious life, or whether, in a paranormal sense, the deceased has purposefully returned to warn the dreamer is a matter of conjecture.

A woman, **M.,** had two consecutive warning love visitation dreams in one night. What is highly unusual is that the visitations were from two different deceased individuals: one, a former lover; the other, her brother's trusted friend. The first dream is as follows:

> *I was in a house with no furniture. Everything is bare, empty. There are green leaves all over and foliage like in a jungle. I hear a bell ring. I go out the back way to see who is there. Two men are outside. They come into the house. One is a servant, the other is my old boyfriend. We go into the backyard. I see birds with sharp beaks. The birds are talking. The two men take pictures of the flying birds. They come to the dining room. My boys are there on the left side. The servant had given my old boyfriend two sticks like Popsicle sticks. He says they are plane tickets for me to leave with him. He says we have to use them in 365 days. I*

say, "What about the children" He says the children
cannot go.

Being in a house with no furniture symbolizes the emptiness of the dreamer's life and the bleakness of her situation.
But the exterior has a jungle atmosphere, which suggests that
the dreamer is in the thick of it—entangled and entwined in
some wild and dangerous involvement. The leaves all over—
in the phonetic rendering of the word—are visual signs or
messages that the dreamer must leave her home, her situation.
Hearing the bell ring is yet another auditory message—a
presage, an omen—and can signify a recognition: a bell went
off. Going out the back way of the house suggests there is reason for furtiveness. The men who come into the house are deceased souls entering the dreamer's unconscious domain.
Pictures of flying birds are also visual presentations that are
given to the dreamer. Flying birds symbolize airplanes and
serve as an additional hint that the dreamer must vacate by
flying away.

M.'s boys are on the left side because they are to be left behind in the world of the living. M. is handed two sticks by her
deceased lover; the sticks are substitutes for plane tickets that
must be used in one year's time and indicate the imperative
nature of the departure—and the danger involved. The sticks
are also symbolic jolts or pokes meant to stimulate awareness,
to motivate and mobilize the dreamer into taking action.

The second warning visitation dream wherein the dreamer
(M.) meets a deceased friend is of similar intent:

I visit my old country house. My brother's friend is
there, but there is no food in the house. We walk the
sidewalks to a bakery. We sit at a table. I have a credit
card in one pocket, but no money. He has no money ei-

ther. We cannot just sit and talk so we have to leave. He goes outside and up a long stairway. He says, "Follow me. We go order." I say, "No."

Whereas the first house had no furniture, the second house has no food, symbolizing that M. is not being nourished, or given sustenance—as food is the staff of life. The warning visitation dream bears ill tidings. The brother's friend is M.'s spirit guide who tries to sweeten the situation by finding a bakery. M. credits herself with being a good friend, but without money she is viewed as powerless. A conversation is attempted but because there is no money the two have to leave—which expresses the same sense of urgency, that departure is mandatory. The deceased friend goes up a long stairway and asks M. to follow, which is echoic of her former dream—instead of flying away M. is asked to ascend a stairway.

When viewed within the context of the dream, the haltingly simple "We go order" is more than truncated grammar, as it clearly demands, "We must go. This is an order." Yet, although this phrase is an implicit warning that M. must leave, she says no, revealing an inner conflict.

Taken together, these dreams make M. aware of what she has been repressing—the desperate wish to change her present life situation, to leave her troubled world behind. (Here, it is necessary to mention that at the time of both dreams an ex-boyfriend of M.'s had come to this country without any money, job, or hope. He had sought her out, and moved in with her. His attachment was most unwanted as he immediately assumed the role of boyfriend, and in his depressed state he became jealous of any rivals to the point where he had begun monitoring her beeper. M. felt threatened by him and even suspected him capable of violence against both her and her children. Therefore, she was afraid to take action against him—to throw him out, change her locks, or call the police.)

With this information in mind, both dreams succeed at revealing M.'s mixed feelings about getting rid of her former boyfriend, in that he is a fellow countryman and someone she has come to fear. This is why in the second dream she does not attempt to follow her brother's friend up the staircase—for what is unknown or unseen is perceived as frightening. Yet, both dreams clearly indicate the sense of urgency to depart from her home.

From a psychoanalytic standpoint, these dreams have a perfect narrative fit—in other words, they make sense in that they reflect the situational anxiety and emotional turmoil of the dreamer. Viewed as actual warning visitation dreams, the two deceased beings have entered M.'s dreamworld as spirit guides in an attempt to warn her of impending danger—she has only one year left!

The following warning love visitation dream of **Larry Geller**'s—hairstylist, friend, and spiritual mentor of Elvis Presley—was dreamt on the day that Elvis died:

> *At the exact time Elvis was dying I dreamt a horrific nightmare that a groaning monster, a monstrous eight-foot gorilla, was chasing me. Every time its claws got close to me I got away. Then I saw Elvis in the clouds, his arms reaching out to help me, and I levitated up from the ground away from this monster.*

Dreams that involve being chased indicate that the dreamer feels grounded in a life situation, but more important often symbolize the phonetic meaning of *chaste*—which establishes that the dreamer is of high moral and ethical sensibility. Thus, the dream contains the wish for justification, self-affirmation, and ultimately to be lifted from the darkness. The nightmarish claw of the monster represents someone wanting a piece of the dreamer. But redemption follows in the symbol of a risen Elvis whose arms or alms (in a phonetic sense) lovingly lift Larry beyond his worldly problems. Larry's levitation is his wish to rise above the heaviness of the moment—running from those members of Presley's entourage who resented his close bond with his friend Elvis. The warning of the visitation dream is to lighten up.

Viewed as prophetic and prescient, the dream reveals Larry's empathic connection to his friend's personal torment and suffering—his timely understanding and perception of Elvis's sense of being driven. For on this level of interpretation Elvis is the one who is chased by his own engorged and monstrous being—with death as his only escape into the weightlessness of clouds. Here, Larry's levitation represents his transformation from the material world to the realm of the metaphysical. Thus, the dream spiritually suggests that Larry visualizes Elvis as both rescuer (savior) and one who is rescued (resurrected). Thus, the visitation dream establishes that Elvis will always be here for those in need.

The following two warning love visitation dreams were dreamt by a designer, **Katy,** who was visited by her deceased mother:

> *My deceased mother came to me and gave me a beautiful green ring. She said, "My sweet daughter, you have to wear this ring. You are too good to your sisters and brothers."*

The giving of a present is metaphorically interpreted as the giving of the present time in that the dreamer is not enjoying her present moments (living her life to the fullest) but rather suffering over her past and worrying over her future. The ring also lends presence to her dearly departed mother. The ring, as a symbol, represents wholeness and the bond or union of two people (as in the conjugal sense) and refers to Katy's wish-fulfillment to bond with or to be encircled by her deceased mother. In that the color green expresses one's innocence or virginity Katy's deceased mother serves up the following warning visitation message to her daughter: Do not let yourself be taken in by others—those brothers and sisters—poseurs of sincerity.

Necessarily, from a psychological perspective, the visitation dream fulfills an emotional need of self-affirmation and support, as the dreamer is presented as being sweet and innocent of the wicked ways of the world.

Katy's next warning visitation dream is as follows:

I am trying to plant a big pot on the ground and I am taking out some dirt from it when suddenly I see hundreds of snakes coming out of the dirt. Then my deceased mother appears and she makes beautiful white flowers grow from the pot . . . white lilies. They are so real that I can smell them.

Once again, the deceased maternal presence arrives bringing gifts, so to speak, in the form of white lilies, which have the significance of purity, trust, and goodness. The lilies are diametrically opposed to the snakes, which signify deception (or falsity), defilement, and evil. The mother has the transforming virtue of turning that which is perceived as bad into that which is perceived as good in a manner that is conducive of Katy choosing to do the same—by not focusing on the snakes but rather taking the time to smell the flowers.

At the time of this warning visitation dream Katy was in the midst of her declining marriage, despairing over whether or not to leave her philandering husband. Whereas trying to plant a pot refers to maintaining the rootedness of her marital relationship, taking out some dirt from the pot symbolizes the wish to forgive the sins of others. But in the process of this attempted stabilization, hundreds of snakes are uncovered in the dirt, making Katy's desire untenable. Katy's mother, as spirit guide and presenter of images, warns her daughter that things are even worse than expected. The white lilies are bridal flowers that are meant to plant the idea of divorce and subsequent remarriage in Katy's unconscious. (In that snakes, as symbolic representatives of the male phallus, are transformed into fragrant flowers, a metamorphosis of strength is granted the female psyche.)

If nothing else, these warning visitation dreams involving deceased beings—with their flagrant signs and omens—provide a strong case for giving visitation dreams the benefit of a paranormal interpretation along with a psychoanalytic one.

The following warning visitation dream dreamt by the Greek novelist, mystic, and spiritual teacher **Foti Kodoglou** seems actually a dream of vindication:

In front of me was a person in a peculiar form . . . completely yellow as if dead. With eyes open he looked at me as if frightened. His face was like a mask, skin, shiny, yellowish-black, as if glued to his skull with the skeletal structure showing. Gasping for air he looked at me intently as if he wanted to be recognized. Then a voice told me who he was and I recognized him. . . . He was in agony, in torture. Empathic, I tried to help him but he gestured me away. . . . He said, "I did not come

. . . they sent me. I am constantly trembling. I want to die but I cannot. Whatever you told me came true. Before I died you talked about religion? Me and my friends were atheists. . . . We thought you silly believing in absurdities. I wanted money and you had said I made a pact with death. I said death would allow me to live long, but I died and lost the bet. I made fun of religion and only thought of material things." Then he disappeared but I felt his frozen hand touching me. I opened my eyes and he was in front of me again . . . smaller . . . like a little baby with an old man's head. He said, "By dawn they will take me back again." I said, "Who sent you?" He said, "There are many others where I am and they are still talking behind your back . . . they are worse. . . . How different the world is from what I perceived. Your truth has won the bet. There is no mercy here. I want to tell the people not to do what I did." Then he vanished. (As edited and abridged from* The Mystic Flower, *translated from the Greek by T. A. Nitis)*

The tortured soul that appears to warn or frighten may represent an unconscious part of the dreamer himself who is necessarily empathic and eager to help—gasping for air he could come unglued at any moment. The peculiar masklike skull is the face of fear which is intent on being recognized by the dreamer, as it is the dreamer's own private torment he fears death, and particularly the afterlife (concerned that his religious belief may not be strong enough to save him from damnation).

Although the very soul of fear is yellow or cowardly, its composition is revealed, as its skeletal structure is showing—but the fear wants more than just physical recognition in that it seeks a moral recognition as well. This is the self-vindicating voice of the dreamer that speaks through the agonized visitor who warns against the evils of atheism. (The hellish visitor serves the purpose of affirming the dreamer's belief—that money will bring man's downfall.) The dreamer is consoled by being told that he has won the bet, that he has predicted correctly what happens to those without faith.

When the dreamer is told that there are many that talk behind his back (but are worse off for it), we realize that the dream moralizes over those that suffer for their sins, yet the warning seems secondary. Questions are skillfully avoided (Who sent you?) by a dreamer concerned only in vindicating himself through the demise of nonreligious others. Therefore, the consoling aspect of the dream is to vindicate the dreamer and assuage his terror of being punished as an automaton who acts out of fear rather than spiritual belief.

30

Instruction Love Visitation Dreams

The following is an instruction love visitation dream wherein the dreamer's deceased grandfather **I. G.** and step-grandmother **C. G.** are able to reassure the dreamer that the anxiety she is feeling prior to the dream is unjustified:

> *I am at a party. The party may be taking place on a boat. There are lots of people all around. To the left is a bar where I notice my grandfather (who is deceased) nonchalantly holding a cocktail in his hand. Then my step-grandmother appears. She comes over to me smiling, happy to see me. I say, "You look wonderful." And then I ask her how she is. She says everything is just fine.*

When asked about what preceded this dream the dreamer related that she had been concerned over a boat cruise that her son would be taking the following night. As the cruise was sponsored by the International Cigar Society the dreamer had envisioned that the boat would be filled with smoke. This thought gave way to a more troubling one: the turgid smoke would most probably make her son (a nonsmoker) leave the smoke-filled interior for a stroll on the deck where he could enjoy the fresh air. There might be crowds of people on deck and by some misfortune her son may get inadvertently pushed overboard. After relaying these thoughts, the dreamer freely admitted that her worry seemed unnecessary yet she still felt ill at ease, until she had the above dream which had the effect of calming her jittery nerves.

It need be mentioned that the dreamer's grandfather was always called by his initials, I. G., and that the step-grandmother's name was Connie. For, during interpretation of the dream, as the dreamer put the initials of the two names together she was amazed to come up with *C.I.G.* (an immediately perceived reference to cigar). Then the dreamer reflected that the party in the dream may have been on a boat. Lastly, the dreamer was able to recount that the deceased couple were entirely at ease and that her step-grandmother spoke the following: "Everything is just fine." This was ample reassurance that all would be OK.

Indeed, the following night the son went on the cruise as planned, and as predicted, remained on deck for most of the cruise; he had a charming if noneventful evening. Thus, the visitation dream may be interpreted as the dreamer's way of calming her anxiety and yet another example of how the unconscious mind deals with everyday stressors. In other words, as mentioned earlier, the dream is the coping response.

A most unusual instruction visitation dream was dreamt by a friend's grandmother (**Evanthia**) nearly two years after the death of her husband. Evanthia had been mourning day and night—crying regularly as part of what had become an obsessive melancholia until she dreamt this particularly vivid dream:

My deceased husband was standing in a rapidly growing pool of water. It was raining tears. He angrily shouted out to me, "Stop it, Evanthia. You are drowning

me with your tears." As he said this, and as the water
level was rising to the point where he could have liter-
ally drowned, a column fell which he embraced. He was
trying to save himself from drowning.

Horrified over the vision in her dream, the dreamer no
longer cried, and thus ended her long period of mourning for
her deceased husband. The dream was therefore therapeutic in
nature, as it relieved the dreamer's melancholia—it allowed
her to stop grieving and crying without any feelings of guilt.
In fact, the act of not crying was now perceived to benefit her
deceased husband who would otherwise drown in her tears.
For the rising pool of water symbolized that the dreamer has
literally cried buckets, that she has cried assiduously.

Taken as a true instruction visitation—as a paranormal
phenomenon—the wish of the deceased husband was to put
an end to his wife's habitual, never-ending suffering. The only
way that this consolation could be accomplished was for the
deceased to visualize for his wife how her tears were harming
him (within the dream).

The following instruction love visitation dream was
dreamt by New York society's most charitable doyenne,
Brooke Astor:

Coming back from China when I was eleven, I felt dif-
ferent from other children—more British than American
because those were the people I saw in China. Mother
was busy, having just returned from Peking—father was
busy with his job. Feeling rather alone, trying to adjust
to my new life in Washington, it was Granny to whom I
turned. She listened to all my complaints and gave me a
feeling of security, making me feel as though I were

*"somebody." Marrying young and moving to New York
I saw very little of Granny, who moved to her country
home in Maryland. Busy running a household—trying
to fit into what turned out to be an unfortunate marriage, I survived, though I forgot about Granny. But
way back in my mind something was haunting me. . . .*

*Then one night I dreamt that I was walking down the
street and I saw a very old lady walking with two sticks.
She could hardly move and as I went up to help her, I
noticed she looked just like Granny, who I loved very
much (and who was now deceased). When I saw that it
was Granny, I said "Granny, I did not recognize you.
Why are you looking this way? You are so thin now and
I remember you being so active." She glanced up at me
and said nothing. "Please forgive me," I said. Finally
she turned toward me and said, "I look like this because
the dead live through the thoughts of the living, and not
you, or anyone else, has been thinking of me."*

This is an instruction love visitation dream of responsibility and awareness of others' feelings, as the dream presents a
painful realization—a young Brooke takes a cool, long look
and chastises herself for thoughtlessness.

When the dreamer meets up with her deceased grandmother, who is at first unrecognizable, self-interest brought on
by an unfortunate marriage is exchanged for pathos, sympa-
thy, and empathy. For after all, the grandmother who had
made Brooke feel like she was somebody now appears as a
cane-wielding nobody. The dreamer's question, "Why are you
looking this way?" symbolizes her utter disbelief over not
having thought about her beloved granny, yet reveals a re-
freshing emotional honesty—Brooke's ability to be self-critical. Not being remembered has weakened the granny—she

has two walking sticks because she needs someone to lean on, or something to hold on to.

What is wonderful about Mrs. Astor's dream is the inversion of the idea behind it—the poetic notion that loving thoughts can make someone stand strong, shine, and alter their state of being.

The following instruction love visitation dream was dreamt by **Ray Adams,** a descendant of John Adams, and John Quincy Adams. At the time the dream occurred Mr. Adams had been mourning the tragic death of a friend who had just been murdered on the island of Mustique:

> *I was in this darkly exotic room. It was a party atmosphere with anonymous people moving in and out. There was really no conversation and my deceased friend Suzy was flitting about. She was moving or just leaving for somewhere. She came into the room with an armful of small boxes—gifts—and she put them in my lap. She said, "I want you to have these." I opened up some of the boxes. There were two Dupont pens and some chocolates. Then she gave me another box of bittersweet chocolates from Paris that looked like sushi. Suzy was dressed all in black and now seated on the lap of my friend Max. He was all in black as well. She had on a bouffant skirt that completely covered her legs and where she was sitting. They looked so happy that I wanted to take a photo and when I turned to get the camera—she was gone.*

As a room symbolizes the dreamer's persona, he incorporates his deceased friend into his room—as she was darkly exotic. The anonymous in and out movement of people represents the ebb and flow of life, living and dying. There is no conversation—words cannot convey the dreamer's sense of loss, which the dream remedies by the deceased bringing gifts. Gifts signify an element of mystery, as they have to be unwrapped in order for their contents to be made known; the dreamer wishes to uncover the facts behind his friend's murder. Yet, gifts also represent the material world, something solid to remember his friend by. The gift of the pens symbolizes the need to communicate or correspond with the deceased; the two pens indicate the wish to both send and receive.

Suzy flits about, as she is no longer grounded in reality, but, rather, leaving for somewhere undefined. Her bouffant skirt covers where she is sitting and hides her legs, which minimizes the importance of walking and hints at another kind of mobility—perhaps she glides or flies.

The sushi chocolates are edible symbols of Suzy—and the wish to internalize or commune in the religious sense with her spirit. The photo that never gets taken is the sad realization that the dreamer will never be able to retain or immortalize the image of his late friend. The memories—like the chocolate—are bittersweet.

The following instruction love visitation dream was dreamt by **Esther Raab,** a Holocaust survivor, at a time when she was in dire need of the kind of confidence that is only induced by love, for this was the night before she was planning to escape from Sobibor along with the rest of her camp. Her dream is as follows:

> *My mother came to me and said, "I know you are going to escape tomorrow and you will be all right!" She took my hand and showed me how I would go over the fence.*

And she said that I could stay in a small barn with hay in it, and that I would be safe. (I escaped safely but never found the barn. I went back years later to try to see if there was one there but I could not find out any information.) (From an interview with Eric Sevareid aired on The History Channel)

In these uncommon, most unnatural, and ungodly circumstances, and on the eve of such a dangerous attempt at escape, Esther Raab must have been angst-ridden beyond belief, fearful of the outcome, of the ramifications from such courageous defiance, and in desperate need of assurance. Yet, pragmatically speaking, not escaping must have been perceived as a fate worse than death.

In that the worst possible outcome would be to die, the dream attempts to minimize the effects of death by presenting to the dreamer her deceased mother, which, in itself, may be viewed as a defiance of mortality. Similarly, the word *escape* may be interpreted as symbolizing two different things: an escape through death wherein the dreamer, reconnected with her deceased mother, will be all right, or an actual successful escape from her victimizers.

When the dreamer's deceased mother takes her hand, Esther not only connects with the loving protective ministrations of her mother but also reveals, in recidivistic manner, the desire to be led. The small barn with hay is a womb symbol Esther is told she will be safe inside. Yet, we are also reminded of the nativity scene: the manger in which the baby Jesus is born. There is safety in Christian imagery, as it represents a symbolic departure from Judaism and from being dangerously Jewish during Nazi occupation. The barn is the symbol of life.

Esther's instruction love visitation dream is viewed as a coping device, as it serves as a rehearsal and imbues her with courage and assurance. The instruction within the dream prepared a less stressed Esther to accomplish her death-defying attempt at escape, as she was confident that she would survive.

The fence (which must be overcome, and which, in reality, Esther climbs over) symbolizes the demarcation line between freedom and captivity, heaven and hell.

This most interesting instruction visitation dream was dreamt by **a woman in England** who had remembered that her husband was in possession of a tape that he had filmed of historical footage of the survivors of the *Titanic* as they were interviewed after landing in New York harbor. He had filmed this never-before-seen tape when he had worked for a movie company many years ago. In that Cameron's blockbuster movie *Titanic* was playing in theaters everywhere, the woman rightly thought that the tape would be well received by an interested public.

But as her husband was deceased she had no way of knowing what he had done with the tape. One night, after many days of serious looking, before the woman went to sleep she spoke aloud to her deceased husband and asked him the following question, "Tell me where is the tape. I have been looking everywhere but I cannot find it." That night, as if in answer to her request, she dreamt the following instruction visitation dream:

A voice (my husband's voice) said to me, "It's in the shed, under the bench." When I woke up I found the tape exactly where the voice in the dream had told me it would be (heard on Access Hollywood*).*

A psychological interpretation would presume that the shed was symbolic of the unconscious memory storage area where the woman would have to go to retrieve a piece of information she had stored years ago. As Ebbinghaus has written, in that memories get covered over and buried under other memories, she would have to go digging under the bench to recall and retrieve what had been placed there years earlier. In other words, the information that the woman presently requests had been processed some time ago and was conscious to her in her frame of awareness which is why it should be still accessible in her unconscious.

From a paranormal perspective, the husband seems to have made an instructive visitation whereby he gained entrance into his wife's unconscious with the express purpose of doling out the necessary information.

The following recurring instruction visitation dream has been dreamt every month for over thirty-five years by the comedian **Chick Lee** since the early and unexpected death of his mother, Viola Mary Lee, when he was a young boy of twelve:

> *I dream that I see my mother standing in front of me wearing the blue jeans she always wore and I hear her voice telling me that she wants me to be the one to look out for my five brothers.*

Chick's monthly instruction visitations are always the same as a way of preserving the integrity and continuity of the mother-son relationship—for there is a control element to the dream within its nondeviating pattern of expectancy.

The dreamer consoles himself by fulfilling his mother's request in that he proves himself over and over again a dutiful son. Yet, concealed within the mother's request (that Chick be his brothers' keeper) is the reassurance that his brothers will not be taken from him like his mother was—for he will keep them.

The following instruction visitation dream was dreamt by **Heather Moore** after the death of her aunt:

> *I was walking with my deceased grandmother on a street in Brooklyn and we were walking to my house. We were crossing the street when my grandmother turned around and said, "Wait a minute, Aunt Jeanette has to catch up with us."*

The instruction of this visitation dream appears to be that death has a future. In other words, the deceased aunt, who had only recently died (six months after the dreamer had a prophetic visitation dream [see Heather Moore] wherein the deceased grandmother intimates that she has plans to get Aunt Jeanette), has not yet reached the level of enlightenment or light of the grandmother, which is why she has catching-up to do.

From a psychoanalytic standpoint the dream reveals the dreamer wanting to reconnect with her past (she is at her old house) and also with her deceased relatives. Crossing the street may signify the morbid wish to cross over to the other side and may reflect a low point in the dreamer's life where there is the wish to escape from routine.

Sometimes the deceased may visit the unconscious world of dreamers, disguised as an animal. The following instruction visitation dream was dreamt by **Candy Van Alen,** whose deceased husband Jimmy Van Alen returns as his former pet. The dream is as follows:

> *I dreamt that a large dog grabbed hold of my little dog's tail. The large dog clamped hold so my dog couldn't turn around to bite him.*

A terrible injustice is taking place within the dream, for a little dog is being bullied or overwhelmed by a large dog while the dreamer watches in horror. Thus, there is a feeling of helplessness. As the large dog has clamped hold, the small dog is prevented from defending itself, which means that no retribution is forthcoming. The small dog, not being able to turn around, suggests that a situation cannot be turned around or altered.

In that the little dog (also deceased) was Jimmy Van Alen's, the dog may be viewed as a visitation from Jimmy himself. (Van Alen created the International Tennis Hall of Fame, continued the tradition of the Newport tournaments, and invented the tie-breaker years that enabled tennis to be televised and become the commercial moneymaker it currently is.) As the deceased can no longer act or fight for themselves they are indefensible, as is the little dog. Similarly, as *tail* has the phonetic rendering of *tale,* a story or perhaps even recognition has been grabbed hold of or withheld. In that the multimillion-dollar USTA National Tennis Center in Flushing Meadows does not display a photograph of the late Jimmy Van Alen, the dream reveals Mrs. Van Alen's frustration over the fact that her husband's memory has been treated unjustly.

From a paranormal perspective, Jimmy Van Alen has indirectly (via dog symbol) entered the dreamworld of his wife to remind her of this slight to his memory in the hopes that she may be sufficiently motivated to finally remedy the situation by placing a few calls to the higher ups of the USTA—by not letting the situation rest until resolved to his satisfaction.

31

Inspiration Love Visitation Dreams

No doubt, inspirational knowledge may be etched into the obscure pages of our psyche yet be unintelligible to our conscious minds. And under these conditions, we usually remain content to trustfully align ourselves with the commonly held view of the moment. However, as the reforming of ideas is known as progress, anything ideationally new that moves away from the traditional may be deemed creative inheritance, an inheritance founded on inspirational thought.

Inspirational visitation dreams may be defined as dreams wherein deceased personages dispense enlightened views that allow dreamers to acquire or voraciously consume, during sleep, a higher learning or inventiveness.

The following inspirational visitation dream was dreamt by a woman (**Mrs. L.**) who had just separated from her husband and was feeling the brunt of the schism. She was worrying about her financial security. Before going to sleep she had sat up a good part of the night wondering about her future plans. Finally, at four in the morning the following dream began.

I dreamt that men were wearing nail polish, but the shades were manly. There was a black color named Panther and a brown color named Crocodile. There was also a gold shade named Goldfinger. I was at a dance club where a big band was playing. Louis Armstrong was there and he had his nails painted in this gold shade while he was playing his saxophone. The color gold looked wonderful on his dark skin. My deceased grandfather walked over to me and said, "You like it? It's called Male-Polish." I was so amazed by the great name that I immediately awakened and wrote down all I had dreamt.

In that nail polish is applied to nails not only as a beauty and fashion statement but also as a measure of protection, the male polish symbolizes that men are already protected in a lacquered financial world of surface patina and veneer that even today still panders to men. Interestingly, the names of the manly colors are all those of predators.

The word *polish* signifies the wish to shine yet also incorporates the desire to become perfected—or to perfect or polish off an idea. A big band plays music, as there is cause to celebrate—the name and idea has been inspired by a muse, the dreamer's deceased grandfather. The colors that start out as dark but end in a gold shade indicate an upswing in the dreamer's mood.

By necessity, perhaps the dreamer was able to reach inside her unconscious into a realm of creativity open to us all to fathom something new that would net her financial security. As security was on her mind, and in that security is associated with protection, a measure of security may have nailed down the inventive product idea.

The dreamer acted on her inspirational idea by having a meeting with Ronald Perelman, owner of Revlon, who, although somewhat amused by the image of Louis Armstrong playing his sax with gold manicured fingernails, decided to pass on the idea, saying, "If I put out nail polish for men all the women in the midwest will not let their daughters buy my lipsticks and cosmetics."

Even though this was one heck of an inspiration visitation dream, ideationally speaking, the concept never came to fruition. Nevertheless, the dream started the dreamer thinking about the significance of dreams, and their muselike value.

32

Prophetic Love
Visitation Dreams

There are certain dreams of visitation that predict future events in a manner so unexplainable that they seem to defy the laws of scientific reasoning. Indeed, many of these prophetic dreams must be interpreted as uncanny. Still, there are those who will try to insinuate perfectly logical antecedents into the dreamer's realm of consciousness as being causative of the foreknowledge that comes to pass.

The following prophetic visitation dream was dreamt by **Heather Moore,** several years after the death of her grandmother, whom Heather never fully mourned at the time of the funeral because she was too involved with her own life:

My grandmother was sitting in the back of a long, shiny, old-fashioned black Chevrolet that looked like a limousine. She had stopped in front of my home in New York to go to a movie with me. Somebody was driving but I did not see the driver's face. She was seated in the backseat, and dressed all in black with black furs and diamond earrings. She was radiant and beautiful. I got in the car and we drove off. And then she said, "We forgot to get Aunt Jeanette." (Aunt Jeanette was alive at the time of the dream but died unexpectedly six months later.)

The frightening image of a hearse is methodically transformed into an old-fashioned and necessarily long black Chevrolet—a shiny pleasure vehicle that drives the pair off to a movie. (The movie, like the deceased grandmother, is symbolic of life based on illusion.)

The deceased grandmother is suitably dressed all in black, but with the prosperous accompaniment of furs and diamonds—as she still prospers (continues on) in the netherworld. The color of mourning is vivified. The car gives the promise of movement to an otherwise deceased and immovable being who appears radiant. Similarly, the movie reflects the movement of reel time, either a continuity of past, present, and future footage or a representation of the fictive, inauthentic realm of the nonreal.

As a hearse is always driven by a driver and not a family member, the image of the chauffeur has been preserved but not without remaining hidden from the dreamer's view—Heather does not see the driver. In that somebody else was driving, the dreamer is driven most likely in an attempt to reunite with her grandmother, whom she had not properly mourned in the past.

When the grandmother says, "We forgot to get Aunt Jeanette," the word *get* remains ambiguously ominous in the dream in that Aunt Jeanette is still among the living. (Here, the forgetfulness may reflect the dreamer chastising herself over having originally forgotten to mourn her grandmother and may signify that the living Aunt Jeanette is suffering the same fate of being neglected.) Yet, in that the word *get* may be substituted with the word *take*—as in take to the movies—we may interpret this word as a reference to the future death of Jeanette.

The prophetic element of the dream lies in the premature demise of Aunt Jeanette who dies unexpectedly within six months of the dream. The consolation element of the dream is that the dreamer has not been forgotten by her grandmother, whereas Aunt Jeanette has.

The following is an example of a predeath prophetic visitation dream dreamt by **Ghislaine Absy** a year before the death of a friend whom she had a love/hate relationship with:

> *I dreamt that my friend was in a tomb underneath a huge cathedral with arcades and columns. There were columns everywhere. Nothing was there but the casket. He came out of it with a white sarong around his waist . . . very skinny and bony like a skeleton. He came over to me and spit on me. (In reality my friend got sick a year later and died, and he looked exactly like he did in the dream.)*

In this prophetic visitation dream the dreamer is visited by her deceased friend before he is deceased, which leaves us with the following question: Does this knowledge emanate from the predeceased via his projected thought into the dreamer's unconscious or is the information already intuitively present within the unconscious dreamer? Or, is this a random coincidental occurrence?

From a psychoanalytic perspective, there are no coincidences. In addition, the dreamer may well have used a symbol of projection to symbolize her own projection. In other words, when the dreamer's friend spits, he becomes a spitting image—a perfect likeness or counterpart of the dreamer herself. Moreover, the act of expectorating means that something internal is being spewed out or ejected externally: the dreamer's buried unconscious rises up from the casket into consciousness. Yet, this part of the dreamer that has been enshrined and encased has come out of its concealment only to be self-vilified by the spit of a friend (who is simultaneously both Ghislaine and her friend) with whom she has a love-hate relationship.

Along this line of reasoning, the friend, taken as himself, who is presented as a Jesus figure (skinny and bony in white sarong), resurrects himself from the casket of death in what would be interpreted as a manifestation of his pure transcendence of spirit. But whereas a beneficent blessing would be in order, the friend maliciously judges Ghislaine by spitting in what must be considered her desire for self-vilification. This may have followed from her loss of faith, or faith in the life of a friendship.

Whereas the many columns indicate Ghislaine's wish to be supportive of her friend (the love part of the relationship), being nonsupportive would make her feel guilty. Her feelings of guilt would turn into a hatred that would be projected outward onto her friend, who manifests this hate through his spit.

In a paranormal view, the dreamer's unconscious has connected with the presentiment of her friend's emaciation and forthcoming death from AIDS. Interestingly, the projectile spit, when viewed as the transmission of a bodily fluid, may be interpreted as Ghislaine's wish to join with her friend through contagion.

PART VII

**Love Dreams:
Relationship
Breakups
of Former
Lovers**

Dream Motifs: Relationship Dreams That Gain Insight into Love Gone Wrong

Dreams are prophetic and interpretative tools of the future and of the past in that they often predict the dissolution of a relationship before it occurs as well as thematically dramatize in retrospect the reason why a relationship has failed. To this extent, dreams are crystal balls that own their glassy futures, and rearview mirrors that reflect upon their pasts—they can either shatter illusions of denial or open up windows of intrusive reality.

Dreams not only interpret the status quo of communications between lovers but they also communicate to the dreamer that status quo. When one acts upon the information gleaned from the dream state one is able to shake free from the fetters of a preconditioned future and is enabled to diverge from a preexisting fate. Whereas art imitates reality through expression and impression, the dream as substitute for art interprets an objective reality of expression and impression unburdened, distilled, or distorted by denial, a reality that can be subsequently changed through an adherence to dream analyses.

The value or effectiveness of dream interpretation is that dreamers are able to reclaim a handle on their emotional lives within the parameters of their love relationships in a way that will facilitate constructive mediation. In that a dream allows its viewers the privilege of gazing unabashedly at their interpersonal relationships, the dream should be used as an instrument of assessment that can qualitatively gauge the nature of any existing situation.

Whatever is behaviorally and attitudinally negative within a relationship is revealed in the dream stream of imagery and symbolism wherein the dreamer is readied, should he or she choose, to fix any problem in the relationship—to alter the prognosis. However, there is a twofold purpose to dream analysis: either sob or solve, either recognize what is going wrong and live with it (accept it passively) or make a plan for action (resist it aggressively) to remedy, modify, or change a lifestyle. Most important, dreams reveal who did what to whom, because denial perishes and awareness is allowed to skyrocket in the dawn's early light.

Like Duracell batteries, everyone would like to have a guarantee regarding the duration of their relationship—to know whether or not their relationship will be long-lasting. There are many reasons that a love relationship fails. Some of the major reasons include: communication failure/incompatibility, wherein there is insensitivity to each other's needs, wherein listening has stopped, and wherein personality, behavioral, and attitudinal differences develop; emotional indifference/nullification of self, wherein there is an ignored mate, caused by the other's narcissistic self-obsession; betrayal of trust/unfaithfulness, wherein there is willful deception and sexual philandering; infringement of personal space/loss of autonomy, wherein there is jealousy, the need to control, manipulate, and own; and unrequited love/lack of sexual satisfaction, wherein physical attraction is either negligible, lacking, or unfulfilled.

Numerous dreams of relationships that have painfully failed (for the reasons specified above) follow, in the hope that the reader will gain insight into love gone wrong.

34

Communication Failure: Incompatibility

THE DIFFERENCE BETWEEN CONSCIOUS AND UNCONSCIOUS MIND: A DREAM DEPICTING CONTRADICTORY EMOTIONS

The following communication failure/incompatibility dream was dreamt by supermodel and photographer **Janice Dickinson** during an ongoing love relationship:

> *I am with my new boyfriend when the paparazzi start taking my photo. I am telling my boyfriend how much I hate the paparazzi, going on about my distaste for the paparazzi when suddenly much to my shock my boyfriend turns into one of the paparazzi. He has this big white camera with a long lens and starts taking pictures of me nonstop.*

This is a fine example of how a dream can tap into unconscious information missed or overlooked during consciousness, as the dream contradicts the present reality. In reality the dreamer paints a glowing portrait and is crazy about her new boyfriend yet within the dream he is unmistakably revealed as being intrusive and insensitive to her needs. There is even a sense of betrayal in that he becomes one with that which Janice loathes, the paparazzi.

Yet, at closer examination the main flaw of the boyfriend is his insensitivity to Janice. Either he does not pick up the right signal or he is just plain not listening. What is certain is the lack of communication between the two—the dreamer is sending but the boyfriend is not receiving. Whereas sticking a camera's long lens into the dreamer's face is a sexual allusion, more important, it symbolizes that the boyfriend's interest is only skin deep—taking pictures of a person nonstop indicates that one is drawn to the surface presentation rather than the depth within.

The boyfriend's white camera becomes a substitute for a blank face that does not interpret Janice's discomfort, as her admonishment goes unheard or misconstrued. Similarly, looking through the lens of the camera symbolizes the detachment of the boyfriend, who is clearly on a different wavelength from the dreamer. The word *distaste* is used to heighten the difference in taste, or the incompatibility of the two.

Yet, on a deeper level of interpretation, it is the dreamer's wish that the paparazzi (boyfriend) notice her and attend to her nonstop in the hope that pictures will help communicate what she is all about (as in, "let me draw you a picture"!).

After my interpretation of the dream, the dreamer confided that her dinner conversation with her boyfriend the night before had left her feeling hurt, as she was unable to convey her feelings to him. (What we have here is a failure to communicate!) Thus, on an unconscious level the dreamer had already found fault with her mate, a fault that her conscious mind was temporarily repressing.

Emotional Indifference:
Nullification of Self

Nullification of self results from having a romantic involvement with narcissistic others who are totally absorbed in themselves to the degree of otherly exclusion. This is not, however, a rejection scenario, whereupon mates are thrown out of an existing relationship, but rather a relationship with self-satisfied, self-involved narcissistic individuals who can only offer a small bit of themselves in the bargain.

A relationship wherein one partner is constantly ignored or nullified often terminates due to a diminishing sense of emotional returns, and a diminishing sense of physical being or presence, in that the ignored party appears to undergo a symbolic shrinkage of emotional status that may be metaphorically compared to the anthropologically severe, physically linked shrinking of the Arapesh.

In this dream motif of love gone wrong there are two variants: nullification of self, wherein as mentioned, narcissistic partners ignore their mates through a lack of attention but not necessarily a lack of love; and emotional indifference, wherein uncaring mates manifest a lack of love and devotion.

The following, most interesting nullification of self dream (which is also a dream of recognition, see Dreams of Recognition) was dreamt by an author after the breakup of her long-term relationship. Both nullification and recognition analyses follow.

> *Nightmare. On subway outing with Vlad. Lonely. Reading. No fun. All of a sudden I realize I __am__ alone. Because he's hiding. He's drinking. It's pointless. He's not doing anything. I want to return him to his mother. I slap his fleshy cheek that I love. I tell him he has to go. Then a pointless discussion with some woodsman who tells me I'm entitled to half of V.'s cabin that he built— that I've never seen—and don't want.*

A dream of nullification is often perceived as a nightmare in that it involves a death of the self. When one is constantly ignored, one's sense of worth diminishes and is replaced by a sense of invisibility, wherein the emphasis is on one's absence as opposed to one's presence. Being lonely while not alone signifies a sense of self-nullification in that the lonely person is being ignored, overlooked, and unnoticed. The word *am* has been underlined by the dreamer in an attempt to reclaim or restore her selfhood.

Within the dream Vlad is perceived as hiding, which defines his invisibility and thus his nonreactiveness to his partner (for if Vlad is not seen, then the dreamer is equally nonperceptible and certainly not perceived). What is not perceived cannot hold any meaning for the perceiver, which is why the word *pointless* is overused.

Just as the dreamer does not want a cabin (Vlad) that she has never seen, so Vlad must not want a cabin that he has repeatedly overlooked and undervalued. The subway symbol contributes to the sense of being underground and isolated.

This can also be interpreted as a dream of recognition. The

sense of entitlement and division ("I'm entitled to half") prevalent among failed relationships even emerges within the obscurity of a phantom cabin that is neither seen nor wanted. V.'s cabin, however, is his symbolic substitute—his persona—poignant in that the dream reveals Jill's lack of want.

The insightful woodsman (Jung's spirit guide or animus, the male presence in the female psyche) reveals the existence of the intangible cabin (Vlad), but the dreamer does not want to possess what is never disclosed—Vlad's essence. Vlad hides to the point of being anonymous, as Jill suddenly realizes that she is alone. (Phonetically rendered, *woodsman* becomes *wouldsman* or *the man who would,* and emphasizes the significance of the conditional in life. Vlad comes along with the cabin.)

The subway outing is an unconscious expression of a submerged or repressed truth. The outing is the coming clean, the admission that the relationship is literally down and out. The symbolic significance of the repetition of *pointless* is that it sustains a nihilist view—the relationship that has already peaked and declined is therefore without a point. A signified recidivist, Vlad is returned to his mother as to the womb. Yet, the one who delivers the slap on his fleshy cheek is none other than the dreamer in an effort to reenact the initial inhalation of life apart from the primary love object of the moment—the dreamer herself.

The following emotional indifference dream was dreamt by the actress **Yasmine Bleeth** during a former love relationship:

I was driving up Mulholland Drive when my car tumbled down the hill. I got out first—then my best friend got out after. We ran to the neighbor's house to get help.

There I saw my Boston terrier dog, Elvis, at the house, being attacked by coyotes, and my boyfriend couldn't help!

A *Perils of Pauline* scenario—Yasmine's life within the dream is beset by one disaster after the next. But what is blatantly missing from the scene is the doting hero waiting in the wings to save the beautiful damsel in distress.

Driving up a hill represents the road to lasting relationships as steep and difficult—there are emotional pitfalls that send one plummeting or tumbling in a downward spiral. These are the ups and downs in any relationship. As the driver of the car, Yasmine is in the driver's seat (the one in control of the situation), which, although establishing her self-reliance, indicates that in order to save herself (and her dog), she must go it alone as no one else can pull off the job.

The house, which represents Yasmine herself, is under attack by coyotes—wild members of the dog family. In a dog-eat-dog world where one can be torn apart by predators, Yasmine has to fend for herself, for her boyfriend appears unable to defend that which she loves.

The lack of caring and devotion of the boyfriend suggests an emotional passivity or even an emotional impotence—he is not able to defend or protect Yasmine as a woman. He is not satisfying her present needs. In other words, the dream establishes that Yasmine's boyfriend is letting her down emotionally. From the very beginning of the dream when Yasmine's car tumbles dangerously down the hill her boyfriend is simply not there for her; at the end of the dream he is there physically but not mentally, which signifies his perceived emotional indifference.

☽

The following emotional indifference and nullification of
self dream was dreamt by **Helen,** during the breakup of a
year-long relationship:

*I go to my boyfriend's apartment to spend some time
with him. He has this huge walk-in closet with big, wide
shelves. We had just started making love when I heard
a loud buzzing sound. He said that the buzzing was from
downstairs . . . it was his doorman apparently letting
him know that someone was coming upstairs. Suddenly,
he puts me up on the top shelf of the closet and makes
me hide. I hear him leave and close the door. He leaves
me up on the top shelf. In trying to get down I fall and
scrape my knee.*

Being in the closet suggests that one is hiding something
from the outside world. Being put in a closet objectifies that
which is hidden (Helen) and is seen as the ultimate nullification of self, of physical presence. Helen's boyfriend has literally made her invisible. By shutting the door on her, she is
shut out of his life. As opposed to a put-down, Helen is put up
(and most likely fed up).

The dreamer's own realization that her boyfriend shelves
her like an item that gathers dust is a potent truth to bear. The
someone that buzzes up from downstairs may be the
dreamer's own unconscious ringing through. Helen seems to
be hearing the door shut on her own relationship as she strug-
gles to find a way down from the top shelf of her enlightenment, where her bruised knee substitutes for a bruised heart.

36

Betrayal of Trust: Unfaithfulness

The following dream of unfaithfulness was mentioned earlier in the text (see The Anxiety Dream) and is repeated here, as it is necessary to reflect upon this first dream of Katy's in order to be able to perceive the psychological dimension of her second, dream of personal unfaithfulness.

AN INTUITIVE OR PROPHETIC ANXIETY DREAM

The following dream preceded the breakup of a Manhattan designer's marital relationship. **Katy**'s dream thematically reveals jealousy and anguish over her spouse's possible infidelity, and it amazingly intuits her husband's romantic involvement with another woman. The dream is as follows:

Looking into the room of my bedroom I suddenly saw my husband. I saw a big white mink coat sprawled across the bed. I saw another woman prepared to go someplace with my husband. I heard her say, "We have to leave." I could not hear where they were going. (Then I was awakened from sleep by the sound of the front door slamming closed. I walked around the apartment and realized that my husband had just left. I rushed to the window and saw my husband with a big suitcase, going into a white limousine waiting on the

*street. He had left for Las Vegas with a strange woman
without telling me.)*

What is fascinating about this dream is its intuitive nature.
The dreamer has somehow sensed the departure of her husband simultaneously with his actual leaving—for he leaves
both in the dream and in reality. It could be argued, however,
that the sound of the door slamming is what causes the
dreamer to rapidly link the sound of departure with her unfaithful husband, who has already, sometime before,
metaphorically exited from the conjugal "bedroom" of trust
and fidelity.

In that a room in a house symbolizes the person, the idea
of another woman must have previously entered Katy's conscious mind as surely as another woman has entered her bedroom within the visualization of the dream. More specifically,
the bedroom represents the marital union. Being outside the
bedroom suggests that the dreamer is beyond the conjugal
realm—on the outside looking in. Seeing and overhearing an
event wherein things are happening without her consent reveals that Katy is in a powerless position. Outside of the marital loop Katy is at best a bystander to conjugal perquisites.

The big white mink coat is symbolically perceived as a
luxury item, which appears in actuality sprawled along the
street, transfigured into a waiting white limousine. Clearly,
the fear of spousal departure from the home was already in
Katy's unconscious, but it took a dream to convince Katy to
put an end to her denial—suddenly she sees her husband as he
really is and is prepared for what is to follow. As the dream
states, the other woman is prepared whereas Katy is somehow
at a loss.

The many signals of marital dissolution and spousal unfaithfulness that seem to have been repressed during the

dreamer's wakefulness have found their avid audience in the unconscious realm of the dreamworld.

Katy's second dream (postdivorce and many years later) appears as a remedial accompaniment (see Retribution Dreams) to the first:

> *I am in my husband's bedroom with another young man.*
> *I tell him to leave quickly before my husband gets back.*
> *My husband comes home. He opens the door of his bed-*
> *room and looks at me with the young man. He says*
> *nothing but merely looks. Then he goes away. He turns*
> *back and looks at me again—very melancholy. I watch*
> *his back as he leaves. On his back is a backpack.*

Whereas in Katy's first dream suspicions are revealed about her husband's infidelity (which are later seen to be prophetic), in her second dream, which was dreamt many years after the fact, it is she who commits the adulterous act. But whereas at first glance Katy's unfaithfulness dream may be viewed as payback time wherein the dreamer is seeking reparations through spousal punishment (she makes the husband feel the selfsame anguish, pain, and humiliation that she had experienced in the past), we find a deeper and different meaning altogether.

By dreaming of herself in her ex-husband's bedroom (the symbol of the marital, physical union) the dreamer wishfully incorporates herself back into her husband's life, and more specifically, into his romantic life. In fact, the wish of the dream is precisely to be caught (phonetically rendered as *court*) as in to be courted again. For when the husband opens the door, he opens the door of the past so that he may look back at a happier romantic time in his marriage (as the young man is indeed the husband) and at the same time look back at what he has done to ruin the marriage.

Interestingly, the word *back* has a duplicitous meaning: the dreamer's frequent mentioning of the word *back* signifies her wish to be back with her husband yet also conveys her wish to retaliate—to get back at him.

The following betrayal of trust dream, which gives insight into a love gone wrong, was dreamt by **Renny R.** of Florida, after she terminated her long-standing relationship with her philandering ex-husband:

> *I took scissors that were more like garden shears. They were so huge that I had to use both my hands to hold them. I took those scissors and cut every tie that my ex-husband owned.*

The scissors as a cutting tool metaphorically metes out both an emotional and physical castration (à la Lorena Bobbitt) in that a man's tie is a phallic symbol par excellence. (That which grows in her ex-husband's garden will be sheared.) And the punishment fits the crime in that the dreamer's ex-husband betrayed her trust by his unfaithfulness.

The anger and humiliation present is so huge and must weigh so heavily within the dreamer's unconscious that she has to hold it with both hands. Similarly, it is necessary for the reparative act of castration to be a hands-on experience.

Cutting every tie is yet another symbolic manifestation of the dreamer's need to become emotionally detached from her offending mate.

37

Infringement on Personal Space/Loss of Autonomy

Whereas infringement of personal space dreams are more concerned with the physical or bodily aspect of jealousy and reflect the possessive nature and inherent insecurity of a love relationship that demands mates to envelop, engulf, ingest, and/or suffocate their partners, loss of autonomy dreams are more concerned with the mental aspects of control, manipulation, and ownership, as they represent the loss of one's personal freedom of choice, will, and decision-making capabilities while reflecting the regulating nature of a virtually powerless and weak-egoed mate.

Just as every relationship needs space to grow and develop, so interpersonal space within the relationship is needed to maintain the integrity of one's individuality and sense of self as an autonomous and independent being. As personal freedom is based on mutual respect and trust, it is viewed as a necessary element of any successful relationship. One who violates another's private space is like a dictator who wants more land to call his or her own and thereby affirm and extend his or her own image.

The following dream mentioned earlier in the text as a negative survival dream may also be viewed as an example of negative self-affirmation, wherein a personal affirmation is achieved at the expense, detriment, demoralization, or minimization of another individual, and also an infringement of personal space dream. This infringement on personal freedom dream was dreamt by an ex-husband **(Mr. B.)** of a former patient of mine who had relayed his dream to my patient while he was still her fiancé. We need to remention that the day before the dream my patient had asked him to assist her in moving from her apartment. He had helped her load up shopping carts with objects from her home. This was the day residue of the dream that the ex-husband (at the time fiancé) hastened to tell my patient—as he claimed that this dream of his was what convinced him of his love for her. Mr. B.'s dream is as follows:

> *I dreamt that you were in a shopping cart and that you were blind and I was pushing you around.*

Looking at this dream as concealing the wish to infringe on another's personal space, the interpretation stands the same as was previously mentioned (p. 63).

The symbol of the shopping cart is twofold: it suggests a constrictive cage and at the same time objectifies the fiancée into an item pulled from a shelf. Imprisoning someone in a cart is an extreme example of an infringement on personal freedom. Being blind further diminishes the autonomy of the fiancée, who is viewed as being helpless, dependent, and in need of guidance and direction. She cannot see and therefore has no insight into the situation, the cramped space she has gotten herself into.

The wheels of the cart indicate the immobility of her legs—her entrapment. The dreamer (the husband-to-be) is the one in control, the one who is doing the steering, the one who is pushing her around, which seems the dreamer's actual wish—to push his fiancée around. The dream self-empowers the dreamer at the demise of his fiancée's ability to fend for herself and is an indication of what can be expected in the ensuing relationship.

In reality, time would prove the dreamer (the husband) an extremely controlling and manipulative individual, one who became both verbally and physically abusive. Had my patient interpreted her fiancé's dream correctly she would never have married and would have avoided the difficult and painful experience of a divorce.

The following infringement of personal space dream was dreamt by the actress **Debbie Reynolds** during a romantic involvement:

I am walking alone on the beach. The waves are coming in, and one of them turns into a huge envelope that threatens to swallow me up. I awaken before this can happen.

Walking alone on the beach is a wish that represents the independence of the dreamer looking to get away from society in general, to find peace and solitude. But even in this secluded spot Debbie is on the verge of being swallowed up by the waves coming in, encroaching upon her personal space, especially the wave that turns into a huge envelope. (In light of Ms. Reynolds's fame, the waves may symbolize the greetings from fans who may be deemed threatening suitors.) The envelope is something that covers one over and seals one up.

The symbol of the envelope becomes more profound in that it is a play on words; the dreamer fears that she will be enveloped by an all-encompassing romantic relationship that threatens to swallow up or engulf her persona. (A word association with a double meaning represents an underlying idea or intention that the unconscious mind is trying to reveal, and reflects the imaginative nature of the dreamer.) Thus, the content of the envelope in the dream may be read in McLuhanesque manner: if the medium is the message, the message of the dream is that the dreamer is looking for deliverance.

The envelope, as a symbol for mail, represents the male gender and suggests that Debbie feels overwhelmed by her male suitor of the moment. Thus, there may be the disguised wish to be rescued, swallowed up, or swept away from all forms of intrusion—for anything that comes out of the water symbolizes birth or rebirth and is often connected to rescue fantasies.

The following loss of autonomy dream was dreamt by **Elaine** several months after her engagement. The relationship failed and the engagement was broken off.

> *I am standing in line with thousands of others, waiting to proceed to a table where military men are taking all our belongings. We are all captives of some dictatorship or military coup. I have a pearl necklace with a big diamond attached to it. I rip the big diamond off and stash it in my pocket. I give the man just the necklace. They take my mink coat and all my possessions. I say to some friend, "Isn't it amazing how before this you could walk down the street and feel perfectly free and now we are watched and controlled."*

To be standing in a line has the distinct sense of being kept in line, which already suggests an infringement of personal freedom wherein one's individual and personal choices are carefully monitored and guarded against. One's decision-making privileges are held in check. Being stripped of all one's belongings is yet another lucid symbol of loss of identity and individuality. The military men represent the emergence of the authoritarian nature of the dreamer's relationship with her fiancé wherein she feels as though she is held captive by a controlling and manipulating personality.

The pearl necklace is the luminous persona of the dreamer, which may symbolize a leash that she hands over to the man in control, as if to be led. Yet, as the diamond is ripped off in a heroic effort to maintain some level of individual sparkle and brilliance (which will have to be hidden or stashed out of view in the dreamer's pocket) it is clear that the dreamer will not fully negotiate with the oppressor. Detaching the diamond from the necklace also symbolically reflects the dreamer's future breaking off of her engagement.

Within the dream the sense of autonomy is valued as a precious diamond to be protected at all costs. Fortunately, the dreamer is able to perceive that her autonomy is being threatened—somehow a sense of self-possession and personal freedom has amazingly been traded for an engagement of enslavement. Something as simple as walking down the street of one's choice is now viewed as a freedom to fight for, as the dreamer is cognizant of being watched and controlled and contained.

Another clear-cut infringement of personal space dream that ended in a breakup was dreamt by **Jane**:

I am in a bathroom and the walls are practically shifting, tilting, and caving in so that the door, now tilted, will not close. I have no privacy. My boyfriend is calling to me from outside the door. I am very annoyed at being in this place. I try to run up these steps but every-

thing starts crumbling as if an earthquake was happening. I am trying to keep my balance. I am afraid I will not get out.

In that a room in dreams always represents the person, finding oneself in a bathroom with a door that doesn't close (where the door is customarily locked or at least closed) suggests an invasion of privacy. There is the sense that the dreamer is unable to find a peaceful place of anonymity, as she is being called to by her boyfriend. In a bathroom one comes clean and washes away denial; fittingly, the dreamer has a revelation: there is the sense that she is being watched and that the sanctity of her space is being violated.

Similarly, when walls break down, solidity is crumbling— there is nothing left to hold up the roof. Thus, whereas walls generally offer secluded enclosures, the walls within the dream cannot be depended upon for privacy, as they are tilting and caving in. The shifting walls symbolize the crumbling framework of the relationship, where the dreamer's very sense of balance is put in jeopardy. Jane has to watch her step, as the earth (or her world within the relationship) begins to quake as if to swallow her up.

38

Lack of Sexual Satisfaction: Unrequited Love

The partner who recognizes that his or her love is unrequited has already come to understand that the love within the relationship is entirely one-sided, which means, in effect, that the love rapturously given is not returned—in other words, a sad reversal of the Beatles line from the song "The End": the love they take is *not* equal to the love they make. Many times, however, this unrestrained selfless giving form of love (as in the romantic Goethe-esque hermeneutic) is sufficient to sustain the relationship in that the loving mate feels privileged merely to be able to love for love's sake, without the need to receive romantic feedback or a refund of the love energy spent.

Yet, there is often the unconscious hope that the situation will change over time, or that the abundant love selflessly bestowed will eventually overwhelm or give way to similar feelings in the unloving partner. But when this does not occur, an incurable frustration or lament might evolve that would bring about the termination of the relationship.

The following unrequited love dream was dreamt by the author **Jennifer Belle,** during the breakup of a year-long relationship:

I felt [the dream] inside my chest. [There was] a building, a sort of monument in the middle of New York, like

*some kind of grand kissing tower in Coney Island. But
it is architecturally fantastic [with] many floors. The
floors were made of fast-moving water, water moving so
fast you could actually walk on it. And we were safe
there, chosen, protected, because we were privileged.
There were men in a conference room, a suite, Robert
DeNiro [and] Al Pacino.*

Because of the overabundance of what at first sight looks
like positive dream imagery it seems necessary to mention
that the dream was dreamt during the breaking-up period of a
romantic relationship. Yet, the role of the positive symbolism
is to allow the dreamer to feel safe and protected in the monument she creates within the dream's architectural structure.

As the dream is felt inside of the dreamer's chest, the
building within (which always represents the dreamer) is per-
sonalized as a kissing tower—a monument of the heart, love,
and the emotions. The dream essentially describes Jennifer's
heart as a monument of unconditional love in the Christian
sense of the ideal, in that religious symbolism is abundant. An
obvious martyr figure, the dreamer is able to walk on water
("The floors were made of fast-moving water, water moving
so fast you could actually walk on it."). The floors may symbolically refer to the dreamer's flaws—her ultimate goodness,
her desire to resurrect the otherwise unstable watered-down
structure of her failing relationship, her transformation into a
kissing tower of abundant love, and her denial that she is losing her boyfriend. In trying to master the adversity within the
relationship the dreamer stays afloat instead of drowning,
feels safe even though the ground they walk on is liquid (not
solid foundation).

The dreamer envisions herself as privileged in that she has
erected a safe domain: her space is shared with powerful,

heroic, protecting male figures such as DeNiro and Pacino who are positioned within a suite (phonetic—*sweet*) of the dream to confer about the best way to ensure the security of the household; wouldn't it be sweet if Jennifer's love involvement with her current boyfriend would stand the test of time?

The following lack of sexual satisfaction dream was dreamt by **Dennis** during the breakup of his romantic involvement:

> *I am dictating something to my girlfriend, who is seated at the typewriter. Somehow I confuse her with my secretary. She is playing with the keys and is making many mistakes and typos. It seems she cannot get it right. She types it all wrong until I realize that she is the wrong typist. Finally, I get frustrated and call a professional typist in.*

The use of the word *dictating* is at once a strong sexual image of the willful phallus and also a conveyor of the dreamer's need to control the sexual situation. The girlfriend is viewed as compliant but inadequate in that she is mistakenly confused as the dreamer's secretary and positioned in the passive and subservient role of taking orders from a superior who stands above his seated employee.

Playing with the keys is yet again a sexual allusion to fondling that has gone awry, as the girlfriend makes many mistakes. Satisfaction is not to be had, as she cannot get it right. Similarly, as typing is done with the hands, the girlfriend is visualized as not having the right touch.

When the dreamer realizes that this is the wrong typist he makes a most ingenious symbolic recognition: his girlfriend is the wrong type. In that she is not his type he calls for a professional (symbolic prostitute ideation), for someone to come over (pun intended) in order to get the job done. Sexually frustrated, the dreamer's needs are not being met.

Another lack of sexual satisfaction dream was dreamt by **Jerry** just before his relationship ended:

> *I am sitting naked on the outermost edge of my bed. My girlfriend is sitting opposite me on the other side of the bed. I am thirsty. I reach for my glass on the nightstand but to my surprise the glass is empty. Then I awakened.*

Positioning oneself on the outermost edge of the bed already reveals the dreamer's wish to extricate himself, to leave the bed or leave the sexual dimension of his relationship, which has a certain edge. He wants to put as much distance as physically possible between himself and his lover. Similarly, as the bed is where one lies, Jerry is on the outermost edge of a lie. But the dream manages to cut through self-deception as it reveals that his girlfriend is opposite him (from his sexual taste or preference) and is even on the other side.

Although thirsty (his desire that needs to be satisfied or gratified), the dreamer is surprised to find that his glass is empty. The empty glass is a symbolic euphemism for the ejaculated phallus (penis) which may or may not (in this pre-Viagra dream) signal a prevailing impotency or premature ejaculation as caused by a physical and/or psychological problem. Yet, the empty glass may also signify the dreamer's lack of sexual arousal.

At the end of the dream Jerry mentions, "Then I awakened," which reveals his recognition of the sexual problems in his relationship.

The following unrequited love dream was dreamt by **Lisa** during a new relationship:

> *I dream I am at my manicurist's salon getting my nails done when she gives me a black and white glossy signed photograph (like a photograph of a movie star) that my boyfriend dropped off for me. The photo is of himself and a pair of shoes.*

The manicurist is a symbolic representation of one who cures one of a man, as she is the analytic presence within the dream and the deliverer of a photograph that tells the whole picture about what is really going on in the dreamer's love relationship. The glossy boyfriend's picture reveals to what extent the dreamer unconsciously idolizes or worships her boyfriend as a larger than life movie star.

As shoes are made for walking, the shoes symbolize the dreamer's fear that her boyfriend will be leaving her or walking away in the future. There is also the negative sense of being walked over. The picture is signed and delivered and may as well be sealed, as a revelation seems to have been nailed down in Lisa's unconscious—the shoe, which has the phonetic rendering of *shoo* or *dismissal* (which is given in plural in the photo) reveals that the boyfriend is giving shoos. This signifies that Lisa has fears of being shooed away by her boyfriend in the dismissive manner indicative of unrequited love.

Another dream of unrequited love was dreamt by **Monte** the night before the first anniversary of his love relationship, which ended shortly thereafter:

In the subway coming home I remember that it is my anniversary. I run to the florist and buy a huge bouquet of flowers with dozens of red roses. It is difficult to hold and almost drops from my hands. I am worried I will mess up the bouquet. I come home but find I am all alone. In the kitchen something is cooking on the stove, but my girlfriend is nowhere to be found.

The subway as a symbol of that which is underground often symbolizes the unconscious mind of the dreamer, which is usually the breeding ground of revelations. The dreamer remembers his anniversary in a way that shows his fear that he will not have another anniversary. The huge bouquet of flowers the dreamer finds difficult to hold is his relationship with his girlfriend. His girlfriend, who is as ephemeral as the roses, is perceived as hard to hold on to. Similarly, messing up the bouquet is a euphemism for ruining the romantic relationship.

At home the dreamer finds himself alone, which signifies that the bird has already left the nest—in other words, the girlfriend has already left the dreamer's sense of self, his private world. Ironically, the dreamer finds precisely what he has lost. His gift of flowers is not reciprocated or even made known, as his girlfriend is absent from the scene. Something is cooking indeed—the dreamer's feeling of unrequited love.

39

Atypical Relationship Love Dreams

There are two forms of atypical relationship love dreams: eradication of breakup dreams that wistfully gloss over past problems of broken relationships and make them reappear as solid (see Frank), and unaware love dreams of former friends, wherein dreamers pair themselves with someone unexpected from their past whom they never see and were never aware they liked (see Susan).

Both forms of love dreams are emotionally insightful: In the first form the dreamers rewrite their personal scripts, and former love interests are incorporated back into their lives (like in a typical Hollywood movie replete with sunset finale) in what would seem to reveal their unconscious wish to start over. Yet, interpretations may prove these dreams only wistful pieces of nostalgia in that the dreamers' present love lives may not be up to snuff. Thus, we have the phenomenon of former lovers returning via the dreamworld to emotionally impoverished dreams merely for nourishment—because the refrigerator is empty and the unconscious mind is hungry for emotional gratification. Indeed, the dreamers have love on their minds, but not necessarily for their ex.

In the second form of unaware love dreams the dreamer is faced with repressed thoughts wherein the love instinct is often made known in terms of conflicted desires—in past consciousness the dreamer was most likely unable (in term of appropriateness) to express romantic thoughts toward an individual (who may have been discounted in the past) who unexpectedly, within the action of the dream, suddenly becomes a hot property worth pursuing.

Sometimes these dreams bring about a significant change or revelation of heart that sends dreamers off on a quest to ferret out their old acquaintances.

The following eradication of breakup love dream was dreamt by **Frank,** several years after his marriage ended in divorce:

I was on a sandy white beach. The sunlight was so bright that it was blinding. Everything was white. The blanket, my wife's bathing suit, and my swim trunks. There were huge palm trees. Two palms were nestled together, and the two of us . . . we were lying on the blanket kissing for what seemed hours.

In that everything is white, the dreamer is literally whitewashing a former unpalatable situation. The slate is blanched, wiped clean. The sandy beach reflects the sands of time and the dreamer's wish to return to a happier sunlit time in his life. Whereas the sunlight is blinding (in that the dreamer, like Oedipus, does not want to see his past) an element of nonbelievability enters the dream; even on an unconscious level, the dreamer knows that he is lying (deceiving himself) on the blanket while he is kissing his ex-wife.

The two palms that were nestled together poignantly symbolize two hands in prayerful position; this reveals the emotional sincerity of the dreamer and may even indicate his wish for forgiveness. The words *for what seemed hours* (phonetically rendered as *ours*) are phrased in a manner that emphasizes the dreamer's lack of certainty of perception. Things are not always as they seem: the dreamer had thought there was a unity between himself and his former wife that only *seemed* but never actually was.

The palm trees (which symbolize the phallus) are huge in a self-affirmation of the dreamer's manhood and because there is still a sexual desire present in the dreamer.

The following unaware love dream of a former friend was dreamt by **Susan** during a lull in her love life:

> *I am in my old childhood home. I wander around and into my bedroom, which looks exactly how it looked then. But I notice some silver picture frames on a small table next to my bed that I never noticed before. One particularly attractive frame catches my eye. As I pick it up I am shocked to find a photo of a former male friend of mine who I used to know in reality.*

Being in one's childhood home indicates a nostalgia and the wish to return to a simpler period in one's life, yet also suggests the need to redo or start again from scratch. The bedroom represents love matters of the heart. Wandering into this room suggests the need to reexamine or reflect upon one's emotional feelings and/or love life.

The picture frame that is noticed that was never noticed before signals a revelation is at hand. The frame, which is viewed as attractive, is a real eye-catcher as it holds the photograph of an unexpected male friend from the dreamer's past. In that the picture frame is placed next to the dreamer's bed it is likely that the person in the frame is one the dreamer desires near her—someone she feels close to and cares for.

Yet, the dreamer is shocked to find a photo of a former friend ensconced in the attractive frame. This suggests that perhaps in the dreamer's present frame of reference her former chum is looking mighty good.

The dream also reveals that the dreamer has grown emotionally and is looking at things differently. Importantly, this unaware love dream validates how we oftentimes miss or undervalue what is right under our noses for the asking.

Another unaware love dream was dreamt by **Tony** about a former acquaintance that he had met under the difficult situation of a court hearing:

I was in the desert near an oasis. A beautiful veiled woman appears. She walks over to me as if she knows me. We are looking at each other intently. I want to kiss her so she drops her veil. I am shocked . . . she is someone I recognize, but someone I never liked.

Being in the desert indicates a dry spell or lull in the dreamer's love life wherein the wish is for an oasis in the form of a beautiful veiled woman. The dropping of the veil symbolizes recognition is at hand—in this case, the recognition that given the right atmosphere (change of setting), a woman previously disliked can become extremely desirable.

PART VIII

Demystification

40

How to Remember Your Dream

As the birth of dreams, their evolution, formulation, nurturing, and maturation all occur in the realm of the unconscious, dreams learn to communicate in the visual language of their derivation—in symbols and images—which is why they are fully understood and remembered by the unconscious dreaming mind. Wonderful! This is why the dreamer has no deciphering or memory problem while asleep; dreams are not foreigners, but rather citizens by inception. And as a dreamer in the realm of the unconscious, the dreamer is a citizen as well. He or she speaks the language, knows the grammar.

But, as we shall see upon awakening, dream recall is made difficult by our lack of translation skills. This is precisely because, when awake, we are all immigrants who have migrated back to our understandable world of consciousness, subjected once again to the daily demands of everyday living, the surrounding stimuli of the senses—particularly the intrusive sights, sounds, feelings, and smells that serve as distractions. Necessarily, as conscious migrants we begin thinking of the day ahead, of plans, worries, anxieties, and ideas, for we are now awake, thinking in the mind-set of the conscious—communicating and receiving input in the vocabulary of the conscious mind, which we understand well. Our masterful ego is in control again, ever watchful and protective, ready to repress any uncomfortable thought at the blink of an eye. But, repression aside, herein lie the real reasons we forget our dreams: Upon awakening we are no longer dreamers; we are no longer unconscious; and we are no longer part of this other unconscious country that communicates through the semantics of the dream idiom—we no longer speak or understand how to translate the dream vocabulary. Simply put, we are without tongue.

In other words, let us imagine for one glorious moment that we are Occidental Operative pals of James Bond who have spent the previous night in China, effortlessly conversing in perfect Mandarin over fragrant dim sum. Our language skills were technologically implanted in our brains via microchip. But, sometime before awakening, we were stripped of our artificial lingual intelligence devices. And while still in China, with maid service delicately tapping at the door, is it any wonder we find we are at a loss for words? None whatsoever. Because we do not speak Chinese, and because we did not take the time and trouble to learn the language. It is like this with dreams.

There is a wonderful *Seinfeld* episode in which Jerry awakens from a dream laughing hysterically. He scribbles down what he thinks is hilarious only to find upon awakening in the morning that whatever his unconscious had found so amusing the night before had lost all traces of humor. His unconscious got it, but consciously, much to his consternation, he is not even close to smiling—he might just as well be in a comedy club in Africa listening to a tribesman comedian telling jokes in Swahili.

Therefore, in order to remember our dreams upon awakening, it is imperative to remain, for as long as possible, conscious in the world of the unconscious. No easy trick, this. For to master this feat we must practice lying perfectly still, not moving a muscle, and not opening our eyes, as this not only limits the commands that the brain sends by way of neural transmissions to the moving of our limbs, but also makes minimal the amount of exposure to the distracting stimuli of the conscious world. For only in this feigned paralytic state may we dreamers begin to mull over our dream, to try to remain in it, and with it, to recap the action—to view the dream cinematically, as a movie we have just seen. Then, and only then, must we rapidly jot down these very thoughts and images on that piece of paper we have cleverly left near our beds specifically for this purpose. Once we have written down the basic script of the dream we may add any accompanying remarks or associations.

BASIC STEPS

1. Before going to sleep, a pen and paper, at the very least, must be placed by your bedside. The pen may be replaced by a tape recorder. The paper may be replaced with a blank-paged notebook exclusively for the recording of your dreams. (A ruled notebook with vertical margins drawn down the left side of each page is preferable.)

2. Remember to date your paper or notebook.

3. Tell yourself the night before that you are going to dream. Speak this declarative aloud. You may even imagine the type of dream motif you want to have.

4. Upon awakening, do not move a muscle. Lie perfectly still with your eyes closed. Ask yourself what you were just thinking. Mull and continue to mull. Remain with what is happening in the dream. Stay with it. Finish it if you want. But do not allow any other thoughts to enter into your consciousness.

5. When you feel you remember the gist of the dream, do

not get out of bed, but rather reach slowly (do not make any disruptive movements) for the pen and paper and record immediately, even in a scribble, whatever you remember of your dream in as full detail as possible. Set down whatever comes into your mind first, no matter how trivial it seems, even a dream fragment. Do not try to recall the full dream, or necessarily the correct order. Then you can free associate and jot down your free associations as well.

6. Be aware of any personal, experiential associations to your dream images, and jot these down in the margin alongside the dream text. For example: You just dreamt of exiting a building. You remember that the previous day you had been strolling the streets of Manhattan's Lower East Side and had made a mental note of all the antiquated fire escapes attached to the exterior walls of old buildings. As it is not far-fetched to accept that your stroll from the other day may have contributed to a dream in which you were concerned with fleeing your apartment, this memory must be written down, as it may lead you to a more profound association. You now realize that the viewing of this image happens to coincide to a time in your life when you are contemplating ending a difficult personal relationship. At this point you will recognize the emotional relevance and significance of your dream symbolism.

7. Focus on colors, the time of day, the season (are you warm or cold), clothing, surroundings (are you inside or outside), placement of objects or people: right or left, up or down, under or above, behind or in front, dead or alive. Focus on dialogue and write it down in closed quotes. Try to remember exactly the way something was said (the ordering of the words is always important to the meaning).

8. If your dream has occurred in the middle of the night, number it Dream #1, write it down, and go back to sleep. Multiple dreams should be ordered consecutively. Any new

dreams should be transcribed in the same manner the next morning.

9.   After all of the above is said and done, reread what you have written and add more associations as they come to mind. Most important, you must be aware of how the dream has made you feel upon awakening, in order to define your emotional state. Are you feeling happy, sad, angry, jittery, guilty, jealous, frustrated, or at peace. Write down how you feel.

10.   Now try to relate your dream to the day residue, the events of the previous day that may have triggered the dream.

11.   Try to categorize the type of dream you have had (see Defining Your Dream: The Three Main Types of Divorce Dreams).

12.   Lastly, try to categorize your dream as one of the fifteen divorce dream motifs, one of the five typical love visitation dream motifs, or one of the five relationship dream motifs.

41

Decoding Your Dream: Basic Steps

1. Always write down what you were doing the day before the dream (this is called the day residue, or antecedent).

2. Always establish the locale of the dream, and the time frame.

3. Establish character delineation (who plays whom); remember that you may be more than one character in your dream, regardless of gender or species.

4. Categorize your divorce dream into one of the three main types, your love visitations into one of the five dream motifs.

5. Try to place your dream within one of the fifteen typical divorce dream motifs.

6. Establish your emotional state, your mood frame (glad, sad, guilty, frightened, jealous, angry, frustrated).

7. On your written down dream, circle all symbols in pen (boat, sun, table, tree, etc.). Then on a separate piece of paper copy down the symbols and place equal signs next to them; then define what they mean to you. Think Associations.

8. Examine the dream wording and underline any cliché.

9. Look for any phonetic associations (blue/blew; chased/chaste).

10. Look at names of individuals who may represent others with the same name; notice initials as well, including the initials of objects, particularly if the object, image, or symbol does not mean anything to you. For example, that big box in your dream may only be there to represent the initials *B.B.*, which might be the initials of your ex-boyfriend or girlfriend.

11. Watch for distortions, wherein something is given major importance instead of minimalized; projections, wherein the subject of a proposition becomes transposed with the object—in other words, wherein we make someone else feel about us what we feel about them (e.g., "I love you" becomes "you love me"); reaction formations, wherein the predicate of the proposition is transposed into its opposite (e.g., "I love you" becomes "I hate you"); displacements, wherein one thing becomes something else; reversals, wherein order or logic is reversed; or word play, wherein names have hidden meanings.

42

Dream Analysis

Many times the interpretation or demystification of a dream is as simple as finding the dream cliché, as the cliché often reveals the theme of the dream. The theme of the dream is useful at first, as it starts the interpretation walking in the right direction. However, the final destination may be one that was not at first imaginable. Sometimes a cliché is not found, and in this case one should look for reversals. The following is an example of a dream that makes wonderful use of reversal.

> *I am in my living room. To the left, seated on the sofa, is Jacqueline Onassis (in actuality, she is already deceased). I greet her and extend my sympathy in regards to her loss of her loved one, Maurice Tempelsman. I tell her, "I am so sorry." She is looking at an empty chair across from where she is seated. I try to console her with the words, "I'm sure he is with you right now; in fact, I'm sure he is seated in this empty chair." She smiles sweetly and agrees, saying, "Yes, I know that."*

Of primary importance to the interpretation of this dream is the realization that a profound reversal of situation has occurred—the deceased Jacqueline is now the bereaved companion; the grieving companion, Maurice, is now the deceased. The reversal establishes the wish of the dream that things be different from how they are in actuality, but also allows the process of displacement to distort reality in a way that is favorable to the emotions of our dreamer—for with Jacqueline alive the dreamer may share Jacqueline's feelings of loss, her suffering and sense of loneliness. This translates to: I feel for her, not him—because he left *her*. This empathic spirit becomes more relevant when we take into consideration our dreamer's former identification with Jacqueline Onassis, which suggests that Jacqueline is a representation of the dreamer. Now that the dreamer has become distanced enough from herself to assume the persona of someone else, she is better equipped to recognize her sorrow and the emptiness of her emotional life.

Because our dreamer states that she is in her living room, death has undergone a transformation and become a live and present entity. Life, however, has been symbolically represented through its opposite—an empty chair, upon which metaphorically rests the emptiness of the dreamer's life.

The symbol of the empty chair has great significance, as it often represents a loved one who is no longer reachable. How fitting, then, that the initials of Maurice Tempelsman are *M.T.*, which, when vocalized, have the phonetic meaning of *empty*.

In that the dream is formulated on an initial reversal of reality, it may contain yet another reversal of just that—an initial reversal. For, by reversing Mr. Tempelsman's initials we are confronted with the letters *T M,* which signify the initials of the long-lost friend that the dreamer had been longing to see. Therefore, the dream wish may be viewed as one of self-consolation, wherein the dreamer has comforted herself with the idea that she is not alone, that her friend is with her in his thoughts and in his heart.

43

How to Interpret Dream Symbols

The following list of dream symbols may be used as a guide to help you interpret your own dream symbols. This list can make no claim, however, to an exclusivity of meaning. This is because dream symbols are complex entities that are literally more than meets the eye, and thus, open to subjective interpretation. Each symbol, therefore, must be analyzed as it applies to each specific dream where the very meaning of a symbol may change or become modified by its relationship to the dream narrative as a whole, to the dream motif, and by how it corresponds with the other symbols within the dream text.

Clearly, in regard to inanimate objects as commonly known as mirrors (which reflect) or windows (which open), or environmental features globally recognized and understood as oceans and trees, there is a certain dimension of universality about which the general public shares perceptive agreement and cognitive attitudinal response. However, even here we are faced with the possibility that many well-known objects are emotionally loaded symbols for specific individuals.

A passage in Jung's *Dreams,* reminds us about the dreamer who dreamt of a table. Jung informs us that this seemingly unambiguous table was one that had particular significance for the dreamer as this was *the* table at which the dreamer's father sat when he chastised his son for being a wastrel, and cut him off financially, which had the effect of forever making the table an unpleasant symbol of the son's worthlessness. This passage also reveals how life situations are remembered and recorded by the brain as if they are audiovisual scenes that were shot for a movie—scenes that incorporate the whole picture, the environment, the images, the moving figures, and the dialogue that determine the mood of the situation.

This is why when we reflect on our dreams we must remember that our dreams have been recalled from our past, a past laden with symbols that are temporally meaningful. We must define our dream symbols and make appropriate associations and be satisfied with the fact that there can be no wrong dream interpretations, for each interpretation represents a certain level of personal understanding, and thus, a hidden part of our self that is now revealed.

APPENDIX A

DREAM SYMBOLS

Above: consciousness

Aisle: pathway, walking down the aisle, spiritual bonding, vows, commitment, dedication of purpose (*phonetic—I'll: assertion*)

Alien: a deceased being, one who feels alienated

Animal: religious or spiritual being, instinctual nature

Arch, archway: rite of passage

Architectural structures: body parts

Arms: protection, embracing love (*phonetic—alms: gifts given in charitable spirit*)

At sea: not on solid ground, without understanding

Awakening: recognition, illumination

Baby: achievement, body of work, creation, creative process

Background: past life

Backseat: being driven, not in control

Backstage: the unconscious

Backyard: your own turf

Ball: sphere, world, self-concept, as point around which everything revolves

Barefoot: baring one's soul, getting in touch with the earth, instinctual nature

Basement: the unconscious

Bathroom: womb symbol, relief, cleansing, bathroom stall, begging for time

Beach: encampment, solitude, peace

Beasts: individuation, breaking away from norms, animal instincts

Behind: past

Below: the unconscious

Bench: permanence, inactivity, to keep from moving

Bikini-clad woman: the anima (female element in male unconscious), goddess as guide

Black dog: instinctual desires, symbol of foreboding death (emotional or physical)

Blanket: security, comfort, protection

Blind: lack of vision, foresight, faith

Blue: the unknown (into the blue), truth, spirituality, sadness *(phonetic—blew: gone)*

Boat: foundation of life, conveyance, boat arrival, rite of passage

Book: of life, self-discovery, pages unread within the dreamer, gospel

Bridges: connections to another world, level of understanding

Briefcase: a philosophy of ideas

Bright lights: fame, blindness, exposure

Broken window: self-destruction, emotional upheaval, inner turmoil

Bugs: babies

Building: the self, creative impulses, constructive outlook

Bunk: unification, steadfastness

Bushes: subterfuge, concealment, submerged sexual urges, genitalia

Calling card: sense of identity

Camel: beast of burden, responsibility

Camp: staying entrenched in youthful exuberance and spirit

Candles: optimism, illumination

Car: drive, inside a specific world

Cartoon: omnipotence

Cashier, checkout people: being checked out, taken stock of, adding things up

Castle: the body, loftier, mature sense of self

Caught: entrapped *(phonetic—court: to date with the intention of having a relationship)*

Caverns: female genitalia

Ceiling: limiting factor

Chair: permanence, solidity

Chalk lines: death, looking for answers

Chased: sense of being pursued *(phonetic—chaste: morally and ethically pure, modest)*

Circle: concept of self, totality, wholeness, timelessness, continuance, mandala

Cities: symbolic of dreamer

Climbing (or climbing stairs): sexual activity

Collapsing: sexual culmination

College course: the course of life, learning, introspection

Columns: body or body parts, phallic symbol as architectural structure—standing tall, supportive, upholding ideals, order

Conductor: energizer, conduit, one who runs things

Corners: the four points of reference in the world, totality, wholeness

Costume: disguise, deception, roles we assume

Coverings: layers of memory

Crib: safety zone, protection

Crumpling: sexual culmination

Dancing: sexual activity

Darkness: ambivalence

Datebook: passage of time, agenda, schedule, self-identity

Deep water: trouble

Demons: primitive instincts, repressed sexual urges

Descending: quest for self-knowledge, self-discovery, the unconscious

Devils: tempters, protagonists, seducers, negativity, hopelessness, falling out of favor, negative animus (the male element in the female unconscious)

Diagnosis: ongoing analysis in dream

Digging: self-discovery

Dinner: emotional nourishment or protection, satisfaction of needs

Dog: Dionyssian animal spirit, instincts, making friends with yourself, foreboding of one's death

Dolls: babies

Door: entrance to illumination, imagination, opening up or closing off, forbidden

Doorknob: phallic symbol

Drive (as to drive a car):   ambition

Driving wheel: wheel of life, symbol of control, responsibility

Drowning: suffocation by system, being engulfed or overwhelmed, loss of identity

Drum roll: performance

Dust: layers of memory, veil

Edge: edginess, borderline

Elevator: that which elevates

Empire State Building: phallus

Empty hole: the unconscious

Envelope: deliverance, enveloped, consumed, sealed off

Excrement: death, decay, defilement, also money

Explosions: sexual activity, ejaculation, orgasm, sexual climax

Extended objects: phallus, full growth potential

Falling: surrender to an erotic temptation, loss of control

Fertile ground: womb

Film: distortion, veiled layer, projection of fantasy, raises identity issues

Fire: frenzied or ceaseless activity, intellect, sexual energy, desire, passion

Firearms: phallic symbols

Floating: on top of situation, above surface, superficial, without depth

Floor: levels *(phonetic—flaw: defect)*

Fly wearing a sombrero: Spanish fly, being manipulated and controlled via drugs

Flying: freedom, renunciation, independence, detachment, objectivity, defiance of rules, exoneration, elevation and ascendancy, establishing individuality

Flying a plane: control, making all attainable

Food: emotional nourishment

Foreground: present life

Foreign city: womb

Forgetting: repression, frustration, fear of loss of efficiency or power of selection

Frog: evil spirit, historically linked to superstitions; something bewitched that was transformed for the worse

Front: the future

Front seat: womb

Frozen: stubbornness, resistance, rigidity, reluctance, inhibitions, fears

Garage: cemetery, graveyard, the underworld, the unconscious

Garden: cultivation of creative side, unrepressed nature, passion, spirit, origins

Glass: perception, clarity, transparency

Glass hall: perception of viewing or being viewed or watched over

God: the father, creator, eternal being

Going outside: independence, beyond confines

Grandmother's garden: womb symbol (that makes a generational skip)

Grass blades: weaponry

Green: novice, unripe, unseasoned, virginal, birth and fruition

Green pasture: affirmative view

Guns: phallic symbols

Hair: strength, power, if cut: castration, weakness

Handbag: self-identity

Harsh light: harsh realization

Hives: anger, physical eruption

Holding back breath: not accepting a situation

Hole: womb symbol, genitalia *(phonetic—whole: complete)*

Homes, houses: the body, the personality, being, self, state of mind (the more palatial the home the grander sense of self), the mother, security, refuge, marriage

Hours: time element *(phonetic—ours: belonging to union, partnership)*

Ice: the opposite of an erection: something that becomes hard in the cold; without emotion; linked to death, in that death makes things stiff *(phonetic—eyes: being watched)*

Incline: struggle, maturational process

Interiors: the mind, introspection

Invisibility: protection, attached to forgetting or being forgotten, unborn

Island: isolation, independence, inaccessibility, autonomy, the individual self

Jesus: father, paternal figure, the good

Journey: departure, death

Jungle: the unconscious

Key: unlocking of higher truth, understanding, opening up

King: father

Lake: reflection, giving surface view

Large audience: the eternal being, judgment, the desire to be heard

Leaning forward: letting go, trust

Leaves: something fallen (*phonetic—leaves: goes away, exits*)

Left: the past

Light: consciousness, awareness, clarity, of spiritual matter

Lighthouse: empowerment, scope, self-illumination

Lightning: bright idea, divine intervention

Little dog: helplessness, the underdog

Looking down: condescension

Losing a pocketbook: loss of identity, sense of violation

Losing a tooth: castration in men, being violated in women, a gap or void

Lynx: animal instincts *(phonetic—links: connective symbol)*

Magazine: the self, storehouse of information

Makeup: covering reality (as in make up, redemption, expression of sorrow), the sense of the imaginary, pretending

Male hostile forces: castration fear, castrating father figure, negative animus

Mask: disguise, persona

Medicine: corrective measures, guidance, problem solvers

Mermaid: anima figure, female element in male unconscious, goddess guide

Mirror: self-reflection, looking for truth, imitation

Mist: blurred reality *(phonetic—missed: longing, yearning, nostalgia)*

Moon: wholeness, luminous enlightenment, feminine presence, purity, ascendancy

Mother: one who births, rescues, creates, resurrects; mother's room; womb

Motorcycle: phallic symbol, sexual prowess, aggressive tendencies, drive

Mountains: obstacles, insurmountable problems, dominating presence, immortality

Mouse: prepubescent male child, phallic symbol

Multistoried structure: multifaceted personality

Music: passions, being transported, sexual rhythmic activity

Nakedness: truth, purity, birth, innocence, naïveté, exposure, origins

Name: recognition

Nature: essence, giver and taker, hostile or docile forces, unpredictability

Nature trail: road of self-discovery

Ocean: psyche, soul, unconscious depths, mother, death

Ostrich: repression

Ovation: approval

Parked car: deceased individual

Party: celebration of life, complicity

Passenger terminal: womb symbol

Pelican: scavenger, hunter

Pencils: phallus

Picture: the whole truth

Pimple: the wish to break out or leave, recognition of repressed anger

Playing: masturbation, motivation, free expression

Playing the game: living

Pocketbook: identity

Point: pinnacle, instruction or lesson

Policeman: the superego, dominating male presence

Pool: the body's internal fluids, amniotic, aboveground pool: pregnancy

Precipice: on the brink of disaster

Pregnancy: filling a void, creative process, body of work (a pregnancy wherein the baby dies: the death of one's youth, fear of responsibility)

Text search: way out of conflict, looking for answers

Ticket: gaining admittance, approval, acceptance

Tiered seats: developmental stages of life

Tomb: womb substitute

Tower: body, aloofness, independence, spiritual or mental elevation

Train: phallus

Train station: departure

Tree: of life, creativity, fortitude, rootedness, phallic symbol, as union of male and female, marriage symbol

Tree branches: offshoots, alluding to evolution

Tunnel: womb

Twilight: neither here nor there, noncommittal, transition

Underneath: the unconscious

Valley: unconsciousness, mother, nurturing wholeness, depression, a low point in life

Video games: at the controls of life, maneuvered or maneuvering

Warm water: tears, rebirth

Water: birth, rescue, redemption, renewal, absolution, the unconscious

Waves: being swallowed up, washed over; waving: welcoming or dismissive

Weather: driving, changeable force *(phonetic—whether: indecisive, physical or emotional condition)*

Wheel: the sun, divinity, wheel of life *(phonetic—we'll: togetherness)*

White: purity, religious devotion, cleansing, truth

White House: the presidency, leadership, self-enlightenment

Windows: the self, the soul, eyes of the soul, opportunities

Winter: death or dying, what is forgotten or covered over, old age, the deceased

Wires: wired-in, connected

Wise old man: guardian, God, spirit guide, animus

Witch: anima, negative feminine side of psyche (*phonetic—which: involving choice*)

Wood: (*phonetic—would: involving the conditional*)

Note: Because certain dream symbols are emotionally loaded for certain individuals, dream symbols cannot be proven to be universally accepted truths. Thus, the dream symbols listed above are those that have already been defined in relation to their respective meanings within the specific dream narrations wherein they appear in this text.

APPENDIX B

DREAM JOURNAL TO RECORD YOUR DREAMS			
Date	*Dream Narrative*	*Emotional Reaction*	*Antecedent*

Date	Dream Narrative	Emotional Reaction	Antecedent

Date	Dream Narrative	Emotional Reaction	Antecedent

Date	Dream Narrative	Emotional Reaction	Antecedent

AFTERWORD

THE DREAM MECHANISM, OR WHY I LOVE DREAMS

The dream, both omnipotent and vulnerable, has equal range of both attributes in an equation of the greatest strength and weakness. Although it is given the green light of authenticity, the dream proceeds with caution, prevailing on symbolic representations to dissuade the awakening dreamer from an immediate dismissive repression. This is because the dream bides its time and readies itself for the interpretative process that will strip bare its visual confusion wherein its quasi-appearance will become a powerful image of credibility.

Our human psyche unmasks this dispassionate yet sophisticated observer, this provocative master of impressions as an ambiguous truth well worth sorting out.